POLAND
NATIONAL HERITAGE

Text
GRZEGORZ RUDZIŃSKI

Wydawnictwo PARMA® PRESS

The Emblem of the Republic of Poland

The National Flag

Banknotes and coins used in Poland

The beginning of the Polish national anthel – words and notes

Je-szcze Pol-ska nie zgi-nę-ła kie-dy my ży-je-my. Co nam ob-ca
Poland has not yet succumbed. As long as we remain, What the foe

prze-moc wzię-ła sza-blą od-bie-rze-my. Marsz, marsz Dąb-row-ski,
by force has seized, Sword in hand we'll gain. March! March, Dabrowski!

z zie-mi włos-kiej do Pol-ski. Za Two-im prze-wo-dem złą-czym się z na-ro-dem.
March from Italy to Poland! Under your command We shall reach our land.

1. Historical outline

The Polish lands fell within the Neolithic group of cultures 6500 years ago, when flint began to be worked here. Layers from 3700 years ago in turn present the Bronze Age, while the Iron Age is represented by the Lusatian culture of 1300 to 500 BC. As one era gave way to the next, iron products were purchased here. Contacts with Rome were enlivened (especially up to the fifth century AD) by the so-called **Amber Route**. In the 10th century, the million or so tribespeople on the Polish lands were finally unified. Duke Mieszko I of the Piast Dynasty was christened in the Czech lands in 966, and the year 1000 saw Holy Roman Emperor Otto III recognize the sovereignty in Poland of Mieszko's son Bolesław I "the Brave". The Polish church hierarchy was then subordinated to the Metropolitan in Gniezno. In the 11th and 12th centuries, the Piast state had its ups and downs, the most serious reverse arising after the death of Bolesław III "the Wrymouth" in 1138, at which point Poland was split into different districts ruled by his heirs. Attempts at reunification under Henryk the Pious were thwarted by the Mongol invasion of 1241. Furthermore, new powers were rising in the north: the **Teutonic Knights** and the **Lithuanians**. In 1295, the crown passed to the Wrymouth's great great grandson Przemysł II, but it was only during the 1306-1333 reign of Władysław the Short that unity was achieved, notwithstanding the Knights and the Czechs. Władysław's son Kazimierz III "the Great" was able to further strengthen the country, unifying and improving its laws and establishing a university in Cracow (in 1364). 1384 saw the title of "King" pass to a woman, Jadwiga of Anjou. It was her marriage to Grand Duke Jagiełło of Lithuania that gave rise to **the Union of Poland and Lithuania**. King **Władysław Jagiełło** made his leadership felt, leading combined armies to victory against the Teutonic Knights at **the Battle of Grunwald** in 1410. The policy of the new (Jagiellonian) Dynasty led to a so-called **democracy of the nobility**. The *Neminem captivabimus* prohibited the apprehending of any knight unless a court verdict had first been arrived at, while the *Nihil novi* constitution of 1505 strengthened the position in relation to the monarch of the parliament (*Sejm*) the nobility had convened. The Jagiellonian period was one of state strength. By the 16th century, Poland's population had risen to 7.5 million, while its language had flowered thanks to authors **Mikołaj Rej** and **Jan Kochanowski**. From 1533 on, the borders were quiet. The Polish-Lithuanian Union was further enshrined at Lublin in 1569, the Commonwealth created being the world's largest grain exporter, among other things. While there was multi-ethnicity and religious diversity, the democracy of the nobility allowed conflicts to be avoided: the 16th century state was that then-rare phenomenon "**a state without pyres**", it was said. When Zygmunt August died without issue in 1572, an **elected monarchy** came into being. Successors to the throne were crowned, having been elected by the nobility at the "field of election" near Warsaw. The effect was to weaken kingly power, and also to increase the role of Warsaw, which ultimately took over from Cracow as capital. Serious problems began with a fall in demand for Polish grain in the 17th century. Economic crisis and military failures contributed to intellectual crisis, one favourable result being the flourishing of a specific branch of Old Polish culture known as the **Sarmatian**. The first half of the 18th century saw Sweden, Saxony, Prussia and Russia doing their worst, no power either Polish or Lithuanian able to contain them. Though besieged by the Russians in the period 1733-1736, Gdańsk held on to its sovereignty. From 1717 on, the Tsar was the guarantor of Poland's "golden liberty", the upshot being that any King selected had to enjoy Russian approval. The last such, King Stanisław August, had done his monarchical career no harm by spending time in Catherine II's bed, yet he managed to avoid puppet status once on the throne, launching reforms ranging from the establishment of the **Commission on National Education** (in 1773) through to the promotion of national sovereignty at the time of the Great Sejm convened between 1788 and 1792. On **May 3rd 1791**, that Sejm **adopted a Constitution** that restored the hereditary monarchy, while modernizing the Polish state. Unfortunately, Russia felt unable to stand by inflicting defeat upon **Gen. Tadeusz Kościuszko** in 1794, thereby bringing an end to the independent Polish state in 1795. The King was compelled to abdicate, and a series of steps saw Polish territory **partitioned among the Austrians, Prussians and Russians**. Napoleon I raised hopes that Poland might be restored when he established the Duchy of Warsaw in 1807. However, the defeat

Stone sculptures in the shapes of bears or boars in the highest parts of **the Ślęża ridge**.

The Penitential Cross of Sobótka – a mediaeval sinner sculpted this cross so as to receive absolution.

Reconstruction of **a Neolithic settlement in Krzemionki,** where flint was quarried for the making of tools.

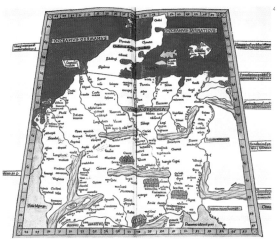

Map of Poland and the amber trail, which was executed on the basis of a description given by Claudius Ptolemy in the 2nd century AD.

A reconstruction of **the Battle of Grunwald** on the site where it took place on July 15, 1410.

of the French ensured that, from 1815 on, the Duchy became an "autonomous" Kingdom of Poland under Russia. The Grand Duchy of Poznań was a client state of Prussia, while the Republic of Cracow consisted only of the city and its suburbs.

A promising kick-start to economic development in the Kingdom of Poland was brought to an end by the failed November Rising of 1830-1831, with consequent loss of any autonomy there had been. The only chances for political debate were then enjoyed by those emigrating from Poland. The January Rising of 1863-1864 ended in failure, and intensive Russification of the Kingdom followed. In turn, a failed revolution of 1846 ended in a bloodbath for the nobility in the southern Galicia region, Austria taking control of Cracow as a result. In response to the policies pursued by the Prussian in Wielkopolska, economic organisations began to appear, these proving successful in the fight for the rights of Poles (to own land and property). The defeats for both Germany and the Austro-Hungarian Empire in World War I combined with the fall of the Tsar to the Bolshevik Revolution to provide Poland with a window of opportunity for **the rebirth of the state**. This was seized and Poland's existence confirmed in **1918** in the Treaty of Versailles. The young country had to defend itself almost immediately, however, successfully halting Lenin's hordes at the Battle of the Vistula of 1920. The Second Republic, lasting from 1918-1939, was a country in which no less than 35% of the population was of ethnic minorities (Jews, Ukrainians, Byelorussians, Germans and Lithuanians). In 1922, the first President of free Poland, Gabriel Narutowicz, was assassinated by opponents at what is now the *Zachęta* art gallery. In turn, the term of second President Stanisław Wojciechowski was curtailed by a May 1926 coup pulled off by **Józef Piłsudski**, whose intervention was justified by the need to rescue the country from chaos. Third President Ignacy Mościcki also had his (second) term cut short – by the outbreak of World War Two. **Hitler's Germany attacked Poland on September 1st 1939**, while **the USSR attacked from the east** from **September 17th**, in line with a secret accord between Hitler and Stalin. The Polish armed forces were inevitably defeated shortly thereafter, the authorities going into exile. The two Occupants set about exterminating people, the Soviets targeting Poles, the Nazis all society and most especially Jews. From 1940, the Polish Government-in-Exile was in London and the country's armed forces were reconfigured in the defence of Britain. When it was again possible for the Allies to go on the offensive, Poles joined the Normandy Landings and proceeded to fight in France, The Netherlands and Germany. Polish POWs evacuated from the USSR to Iran in turn formed a second army that fought in North Africa and Italy, while Poland's communists created yet a third army that fought with Soviet forces all the way to Berlin. Meanwhile, Poles at home had created the underground Home

The defence of Jasna Góra – a turning point in the Swedish Wars of the 17th century, depicted on the ceiling of **a church in Okrzeja**.

Jean Pierre Norblin de la Gourdaine's
The Passing of the May 3 Constitution of 1791.

Visit of the future Head of the Polish state **Józef Piłsudski** to Wawel in 1916, following the proclamation of the Polish kingdom.

Professor Stanisław Wojciechowski, the president of the Republic of Poland between 1922-1926.

Ignacy Jan Paderewski – campaigner for the independence of Poland. In 1919 as Prime Minister of Poland he signed the Treaty of Versailles.

Army and an extensive web of other secret organisations. The fighting, expulsions, ethnic purges and genocides of 1939-45 cost Poland more than 6 million people. Furthermore, **concessions made to Stalin at Yalta** allowed the country to remain in the Soviet sphere post-War. This was confirmed in rigged referenda of 1947, giving the authorities carte blanche to proceed with the establishment of a police state, in which the opposition could be persecuted, tortured and murdered into submission. Ineffectual in most other fields, the **People's Republic of Poland (PRL)** faced bankruptcy in 1956, 1968, 1970, 1976 and finally in 1980, all the time facing the prospect of armed interventions by neighbours. Naturally, the imposition of Martial Law in 1981 offered no longer-term solutions, such that by 1988, the PRL was ready to be toppled by the people. Free presidential elections came in 1990, the winner being **Lech Wałęsa**, leader of the "Solidarity" trade union that had so effectively pushed for change. It was upon Wałęsa that President-in-Exile **Ryszard Kaczorowski** conferred the state insignia of Poland saved in 1939. Three years later, the Red Army made its final exit and the communist era truly ended. Poland joined NATO in 1999, as well as the European Union on May 1st 2004. The country also became part of the EU's Schengen Area on 21st December 2007. On April 10th 2010, Poles sustained another terrible blow in their history. The air crash near Smoleńsk in Russia killed the entire official delegation en route for the commemorations of **the 70th anniversary of the Katyń Massacre**, as headed by President of Poland **Lech Kaczyński** and his wife Maria, guest of honour Ryszard Kaczorowski, the last Polish President-in-Exile, and a host of leading figures from the worlds of politics, administration, the clergy, the armed forces, NGOs, etc.

Furnishings and objects from **the offices of the Polish government in exile** from 1939-1992 were bequeathed to the Royal Castle in Warsaw.

Archive photo of **the battleship Schleswig-Holstein** firing on a Polish military base in the free city of Gdańsk in September 1939.

Ruins of the city of Gdańsk
in 1945 in the aftermath of war and a hurricane.

John Paul II – Polish Pope
and architect of Polish independence. Born on May 18th,
1920 in Wadowice, he died on April 2nd, 2005 in the Vatican.

Lech Wałęsa – leader of the Solidarity movement and the first
president of the Republic of Poland to be elected in a general election.

President Aleksander Kwaśniewski with his wife, Jolanta, during
celebrations of Poland's Independance Day on November 11th, 2003.

Lech Kaczyński, President of the Republic of Poland in the years
2005-2010, who died so tragically in the air disaster taking place
near Smoleńsk in Russia.

A Warsaw street covered with funeral candles
the day **after the death of Pope John Paul II**. This image
was mirrored the length and breadth of Poland on the day
of the Pope's funeral, which took place in Rome on April 3rd, 2005.

The **Katyń Museum** in Mokotów was created to commemorate
the Polish officers murdered by the NKVD on Stalin's order in 1940.
The museum has gathered mementos of the victims
of **Katyń, Kharkov** and **Mednoye**.

April 2010. At the Presidential Palace in Warsaw, Poles **pay last
respects** to the victims of the disaster involving the Presidential
plane, which crashed at Smoleńsk.

The Military (now municipal) Cemetery at Powązki.
This symbolic grave for the victims of the Katyń Massacre
is known as the **Katyń Monument**.

2. Geographical location and natural conditions

Poland (or officially the **Republic of Poland** *Rzeczpospolita Polska*) is a **European Union** Member State located in Central Europe, by the Baltic, in the **drainage basins of the Vistula and Oder**, between 54°50' and 49°00' N and between 14°07' and 24°08' E. It extends as much as 649 km in a N-S direction and for 689 km along parallel 52 degrees N. The line of longitude 15 degree east delimiting Central European Time runs through Poland more or less parallel to its western border, and the point denoting the geometric centre of Europe is located in Suchowola, in the north-east of the country. Poland covers some 312,700 km², and supports a population in excess of 38 million. This is a **lowland country**, in which more than 91% of the land is below 300 m a.s.l.. While the highest point – the north-west summit of **Rysy in the High Tatra Mountains** – reaches 2499 m a.s.l., the average altitude in Poland is of just 173 m a.s.l. (as compared with 330 m a.s.l. in Europe as a whole). The highest land and most varied relief characterise the **Carpathians** – young mountains extending along the border with Slovakia, and the **Sudety Mountains (Sudetes)** – much older features of complex geological structure existing along the Polish-Czech border. North of the Carpathians, we find an associated series of basins, and beyond them a belt of uplands comprising the **Silesian**, **Cracow-Wieluń** and **Kielce Uplands** and **the chain of the Świętokrzyskie Mountains**. In turn, to the east of the channel of the Lublin Vistula there is the **Roztocze** belt of uplands resembling small mountains in many ways. The highest point in the Polish uplands is Łysica (at 612 m a.s.l.) – the loftiest peak in the Świętokrzyskie Mountains dating back to the Palaeozoic. The greater part of Poland is occupied by lowlands incised by river valleys, in which there are numerous glacial relict features including lakes and picturesque elevations formed from glacial moraine. The **Baltic Coast** comprises more than 500 kilometres of sandy beaches, along with coastal lagoons and lakes and even steep, retreating cliffs along certain stretches. Poland lies on the boundary between a temperate climate and a snowy forest climate, as well as between the oceanic and continental climatic influences. That is why there are fairly frequent weather fluctuations and variable lengths of the seasons in consecutive years. And, while the lowest temperature ever noted here was the – 41°C reported in January 1940, the highest was the 40.2°C recorded in July 1921. In line with the climate, the flora of Poland is a varied one with more than 2300 species of vascular plant, c. 600 species of moss, 250 species of liverwort and 1600 species of lichen. Poland's original landscape was very largely forest, though this kind of cover today accounts for just 29% of the country's area. More than 50% is in turn taken by cultivated fields. The largest forest areas remaining comprise: the **Lower Silesian Forests** (*Bory Dolnośląskie*) covering 1500 km², the **Solska Forest** (1240 km²), the **Tuchole Forests** (*Bory Tucholskie*) (c. 1200 km²), the **Augustów Forest** (*Puszcza Augustowska* – 1140 km²), the **Knyszyn Forest** (*Puszcza Knyszyńska* – 839 km²) and the largest of all – though with only 580 km² on the Polish side of the border with Belarus, the famous Białowieża Forest (*Puszcza Białowieska*). The forest type occurring most frequently is pine forest with an admixture of broadleaved species. The animal world is represented by many of the species **typical for the zone of broadleaved and mixed forest**, among them the red squirrel, brown hare, fox, roe deer and red deer. Equally common at one point, but now largely confined to protected areas,

Flat-bottomed river valleys are often found in the **lowlands of Central Poland**. In the photo we see Sowia Góra near Węgrów in Mazovia, a view of the **Valley of the Liwiec River**.

In the **Mazovian countryside** you will often find willows growing alongside roads or in meadows.

The Vistula, the queen of Polish rivers, coursing through Tyniec outside Cracow. Here it has yet to widen to the extent that it does further on down river.

are the golden eagle, capercaillie, European bison, wild cat, lynx and brown bear. The beaver, raven, cormorant and mute swan are all now commoner than they were, having benefited from programmes of strict protection at the end of the 20th century. Most of Poland's inhabitants live in towns and cities, the main concentrations of population being the Katowice Agglomeration with its nearly 30 towns and cities in Upper Silesia; the Warsaw and Łódź Agglomerations and the Tri-City on the coast comprising Gdańsk, Sopot and Gdynia. The largest individual cities are, in turn: Warsaw, Cracow, Łódź, Wrocław and Poznań.

The lush habitat of **the Vistula floodplain in the Secymin region**, located at the north end of the Kampinos Forest, is often flooded by one of Europe's largest unregulated rivers.

Lake Jeziorak, the largest lake in **the Iława Lake District** and the longest lake in Poland, is branched with a surface area of 34.6 km².

The scenery of Suwałki Landscape Park is dominated by lakes, forests and hills. **Cisowa Mountain is** the highest hill in the photo, and is fondly referred to as Suwałki's "Mount Fuji".

Lake Rajgrodzkie in the Ełk Lake District, situated in north-east Poland, has a surface area of 1,514 hectares and a maximum depth of 52 m.

The hilly **landscape of Spisz**, situated in the Carpathian Mountains between the Tatra Mountains and the Pieniny Mountains, is crisscrossed with narrow strips of farmland.

Lublin Upland is built from deposits of loess – a dusty sedimentary rock which rain sculpts into **ravines and gorges, just like** that near **Kazimierz Dolny on the Vistula River,** on the western edge of the upland.

The limestone hills of **Cracow's Krzemionki** have been intensively quarried.

Skałki Piekło (Hell Rocks), a nature reserve near Niekłań situated on the north edge of the Świętokrzyskie Mountains, protects formations of Triassic and Jurassic rocks exposed on the edge of the deep river valley.

Brama Twardowskiego (Twardowski's Gate) situated to the south of Złoty Potok village, is one of the more interesting rock formations to be found in **Jura Krakowsko-Częstochowska**.

The **Club of Hercules**, a naturally formed limestone rock with a narrowing base, is one of the main attractions of the picturesque Prądnik Valley, and is to be found at the foot of **Pieskowa Skała Castle** near Cracow.

Ślęża – the holy mountain of the Ślęża peoples rises to 718 m asl, whereas the **plains of the Silesian Lowland,** surrounding it from the north and east, do not rise higher than 200 m asl.

Jaskinia Niedźwiedzia (The Bear Cave) in Kletno in the **Bialskie Mountains** was discovered by chance at the end of 1960's during quarry work. Picturesque and pristine stalactites can be found in the cave.

The **Giewont**, 1,895 m asl – the line of its ridge is shaped like a sleeping knight. The northern slopes form a 600 metre high wall, which is almost vertical – attempts by tourists to climb the wall often end in tragedy. A friendly tourist trail leads to the peak from the south.

View of the **High Tatra Mountains** from the north.

View of the slope of **Hala Gąsienicowa from Kasprowy** Peak (1,987 m asl) – enjoyed by skiers since the end of the 19th century, to be joined by hang-glider enthusiasts at the end of 20th century.

The surroundings of the tourist hostel at **Morskie Oko** (Sea Eye). **Niżne Rysy** (2430 m asl) is situated vertically above the building, to the right of it the highest peak in Poland (although from this view it seems to be lower). The Polish peak of **Rysy** rises to 2499 m asl, whereas the Slovakian peak rises to 2503 m asl.

At 70 metres high, **Wielka Siklawa** (The Great Waterfall) in the **Roztoki Valley** is the highest waterfall in Poland.

Since ancient times the white eagle has been the emblem of Poland. However, the **white stork**, *Ciconia ciconia*, is most associated with Poland. Indeed, a quarter of the world's population of these birds nest in Poland.

Puszcza Borecka (Borecka Forest), situated in the northern part of **the Mazurian Lake District,** is famous for its roaming bison and boasts linden and hornbeam trees.

The beaches of Poland's Baltic coastline are a popular holiday destination and it's often said that sandcastle enthusiasts have done much to inspire Poland's architects.

A sandy beach stretches **along the entirety of Poland's Baltic coastline**. Holiday resorts are very crowded in summertime.

The steep Orłowo cliff overlooks the beach in **Gdynia Orłowo** between Sopot and Gdynia. In wintertime it is a magnificent setting for invigorating walks, with the sea-air saturated with iodine.

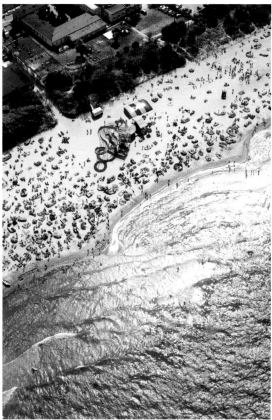

3. Warsaw

Poland's capital is a city of 1.7 million people that co-creates an agglomeration of some 2.4 million. The city is **on the River Vistula**, and is located at the centre of Mazowsze (the old Mazovia). Long a political and financial centre (as seat of parliament, government, the National Bank of Poland, the Stock Exchange, etc.), this is also a major industrial city and Poland's main place of learning. Among the higher education institutions here are the country's largest – the **University of Warsaw**, as well as **Warsaw University of Technology**, Warsaw Medical School, Academies of Music, the Fine Arts, Theatre and so on, and some 10-20 other colleges of various profiles. The role of the capital as cultural centre extends beyond Poland, the Fryderyk Chopin International Piano Competition held every 5 years attracting interest from around the World, for example, as does the annual *Warszawska Jesień* ("Warsaw Autumn") International Festival of Contemporary Music, and the International Book Fairs. *Warszewa* means "property of *Warsz*", where *Warsz* is a diminutive version of the Slav name *Warcisław*. The commercial settlement going by the above name from the 13th century obtained town rights around 1300. It made its first more major mark on recorded history on February 4th 1339, when the case of King Kazimierz the Great against the Teutonic Knights was taken up here. Having served as the capital of the Piast Dukedom of Mazovia for some time, the end of that dynasty in 1526 resulted in Warsaw's full incorporation into Poland. Progress was rapid thereafter, Parliamentary Assemblies choosing to convene here from 1569, the gatherings designated for the election of Polish Kings from 1573. The King set up here in 1596, though the formal transfer of the Royal Court from Cracow only in fact took place in 1611. The Swedish War of 1655-1660 left the city in such ruins that only during the 1763-1795 reign of last King of Poland Stanisław August did Warsaw first regain and then surpass its former glory.

King Stanisław's reign was fest ebbing away by 1794, when Russian forces engaged in a bloody massacre in right-bank Warsaw, only for the whole city to fall subsequently into the hands of Poland's Prussian Partitioners. Capital city status (of a kind) was regained with the creation of the **Duchy of Warsaw**, which lasted from 1807-1813, as well as the Duchy's Russian-ruled successor the (Congress) **Kingdom of Poland**. Academic centre status was achieved with the founding of the University of Warsaw in 1816, while an industrial tradition began with the establishment of the first of many factories in 1824. Having suppressed the November (1830) Rising, the Russians tightened their grip on Warsaw, constructing **the Citadel** to that end. Warsaw had gained a **rail link with Vienna** by 1848, and with **St. Petersburg** by 1862. The January Uprising (of 1863) was associated with the establishment of a National Government in Warsaw. Its members lost their lives in the Citadel in the course of post-Rising repressions. A 1905-1907 rebellion

Bernardo (*Canaletto*) Bellotto's, **View of Warsaw from Praga,** oil on canvas painting with dimensions of 260.5 x of 167 cm, dated 1770.

47

by the Vistula began when workers went out on strike in Warsaw's Wola district. However, Poland's rebirth was only signalled by the arrival in the city of Józef Piłsudski on what came to be termed Independence Day – November 11th 1918. Inter-War Warsaw was indisputably the Second Republic's main centre of Polish political and cultural life, as well as being a world centre for Jewish culture. There was an airport here from 1921, while Polish Radio went into operation from 1926. By 1939, there were some 1,300,000 Varsovians, including 394,000 Jews. The outbreak of the War signalled the onset of a four-stage process of devastation for the Polish capital. First, between 8th and 27th September 1939, the city defended itself as best it could from German attacks by air and land, the targets – and the casualties – being as much civilian and cultural as they were military. The period 19th April to 16th May 1943 then saw the liquidation of the Jewish Ghetto and its consequence, the famous Ghetto Uprising eventually suppressed by tanks and aircraft. The 3rd phase entailed the also-legendary **Warsaw Uprising** of August 1st to October 2nd 1944 – a heroic push for freedom crushed in the bloodiest fashion by Nazi Germany at the cost of the lives of more than 200,000 Warsaw inhabitants. Not satisfied by that level of repression, the Occupant used the period November-December 1944 to first expel any remaining citizenry and then precede with the house-by-house levelling of the capital.

Soldiers patrolling. **The Warsaw Uprising**. August 1944.

Aerial photograph of **the ruined centre of Warsaw** in 1945.

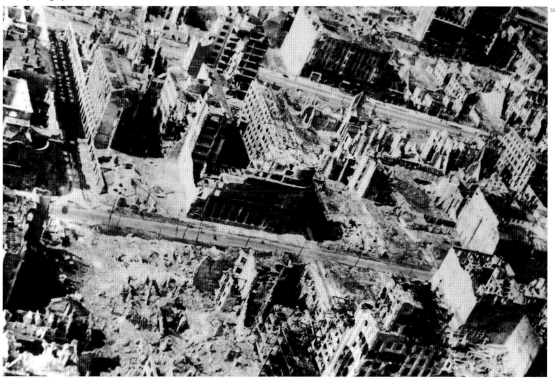

Roadside chapel – fragment from exhibition
of **the Warsaw Uprising Museum**.

Graves of the victims of tsarist rule
on the slopes of **the Warsaw Citadel**.

Monument for the Fallen and Murdered in the East,
commemorating the victims of Stalinist transportations to Siberia
in the years 1939-1941 and 1944-1945.

Guard of honour by **the Monument of the Warsaw Uprising**.

84% of the fabric of the city was destroyed at that point.
Post-War Warsaw offered ideal conditions for
the propaganda machine of a Soviet-controlled communist
Poland to swing into action. Heroic rebuilding work was put
in the hands of "approved" architects and planners. 1949
brought a detailed "6-Year Plan for the Reconstruction
of Warsaw" that was under the personal patronage
of Bolesław Bierut, then President of Poland and
(more importantly) First Secretary of the Polish United
Workers' Party (PZPR). The *de facto* aim was to ensure that
Warsaw took on the appearance of other cities
in the Soviet-run Eastern Bloc. That aim was all-too-visible
by 1955, when the finishing touches were put to two
Socialist-Realist items: the MDM Residential District along
the main thoroughfare of Marszałkowska Street,
and the dominating skyscraper known as the Palace

The Tomb of the Unknown Soldier
in the remains of the colonnade of Saski Palace.

Tenement buildings on the Old Town Market Square rebuilt after the war in accordance with their historical architectural style. The tenement houses seen here are those of the "Barss side".

The Mermaid "Syrenka", whose monument stands in the Old Town Market Square, lived in the Vistula river and defended the settlement of Warsz, the legendary founder of the city, with a sword. Since the Middle Ages the "Syrenka" has been represented on Warsaw's coat of arms.

Defensive walls of the Old Town and **the Barbican**.

of Culture and Science. Both remain in place today. In fact, the 1960s and 70s were to see such ideological pretensions and aspirations set aside as the authorities sought to respond to the desperate need for more housing to go up as quickly as possible. The still-less-attractive results were the mammoth estates and dormitory districts comprising row upon row of grey concrete blocks. Only as the capital of a free Poland could late 20th- and early 21st-century Warsaw again begin to acquire some more architecturally-interesting items, as part of a building boom that has involved world-famous architects.

Today's unique cityscape of Warsaw comprises (a few) surviving old buildings, as well as a large number of painstakingly reconstructed ones. A visit ought probably to begin with **the Park-Palace Complex at Wilanów** in the south of the city, this being the Baroque-style residence of King Jan III Sobieski. Somewhat nearer to the city-centre, Mokotów district boasts the picturesque

The picturesque **Piwna Street in the Old Town**. Visible above the houses by the Wąski Dunaj (The Narrow Danube) are the towers of the Church of the Holy Ghost in the New Town.

The throne room of **the Royal Castle,** whose interior decor was prepared for Stanisław August Poniatowski. The wall behind the throne is decorated with eagles embroidered in silver and gold.

View from the belfry terrace of St Anne's church of **the Castle Square**, the Castle and the Cathedral; to the left the Column of Zygmunt III Waza – the oldest Warsaw monument – erected in 1644.

Królikarnia Mansion located on the Warsaw Escarpment **and home to a collection of Xawery Dunikowski sculptures.** Another former royal residence and estate (of King Stanisław August Poniatowski) is located in **Royal Łazienki Park.** The most famous building there is the **Palace on the Island.** This residence is linked with the **Royal Castle** via the **Royal Way** that passes along the Embassy-lined **Aleje Ujazdowskie,** via **Nowy Świat** Street with its Holy Cross Church holding **Chopin's heart,** and into **Krakowskie Przedmieście Street,** a thoroughfare whose atmosphere readies the visitor for his/her encounter with a faithfully-reconstructed **Old Town** that features on the **UNESCO List of World Heritage Sites.** The Site Designation pays tribute to the painstaking nature of the rebuilding work, carried out with the aid of surviving fragments of the original buildings, as well as pre-War technical documentation and paintings – not least those of **Bernardo Bellotto.**

The classicist façade of **St Anne's Church** dates from 1788 and was designed by Stanisław Kostka Potocki and Christian Peter Aigner.

Chancellor's chamber in **Kazimierz Palace**, which was erected in the years 1626-1632 and rebuilt for Warsaw University in the years 1814-1816.

Inner courtyard of the Main Building of **Warsaw Polytechnic.**

Figure of Christ sculpted by Andrzej Pruszyński, in front of **the Holy Cross Church**. Urns with the hearts of Fryderyk Chopin and Władysław Reymont are enclosed in the pillars of the nave of the church.

It is possible to view **the Palace on the Island** by gondola as it is situated in the middle of a pond.

Łazienki Park – the interior of **the Rotunda of the Palace on the Island** is adorned with the statues of outstanding monarchs: Kazimierz Wielki (Kazimierz the Great), Jan III Sobieski, and, as can be seen in the photograph, Zygmunt I (Sigusmund the first) and Stefan Batory.

Wilanów Palace – the royal residence of king Jan III Sobieski – The Great Crimson Room – the Potocki Family Gallery.

Gate of the Baroque park and palace complex in **Wilanów**.

Above the roofs of the socialist buildings of **Marszałkowska Dzielnica Mieszkaniowa** (Marshal's residential district) (MDM) on Plac Konstytucji (Constitution Square) you'll find the billboards of capitalist companies.

The Palace of Culture and Sciences (previously called Stalin's Palace) built in the years 1952-1955 to the design of Soviet architect, Lew Rudniew. It is the highest building in Poland and with its spire measures 230 metres.

Congressional Hall of the Palace of Culture and Sciences – in the communist era the venue for Party conventions. Today it is a prestigious concert hall that holds 3 thousand spectators.

The Metropolitan office block by Piłsudski Square designed
by Norman Foster; the fountain in the courtyard plays
to computer-operated rhythms.

   The Supreme Court Buildings by Krasińskich Square.
Slender caryatids bear the weight of the glass construction.

   Eminent logicians Alfred Tarski, Stanisław Leśniewski
and Jan Łukasiewicz, look down from the high plinths within
the building of the Warsaw University Library.

   44 Złota Street, or "**The Sail**" – one of the more interesting
developments of recent years, this skyscraper was designed
by Daniel Libeskind.

John Paul II Avenue: the investment in ever-taller buildings not only
stems from the increasing value of land but it is also a represents
Warsaw architecture at the turn of the 21st century.

4. Cracow

Cracow, **formerly the capital of Poland**, is today "only" the headquarters of its voivodship, though this city of 780,000 is still perceived as much more, being for example the major centre of Polish academic and cultural life, as well as a significant seat of industry (making steel, coke, machinery, medicines, rubber and food products). Strategically located **by the Vistula**, it is also a communications hub, with its own airport. The name seems to go back to the legendary Prince Krak (Grakh), and was certainly being mentioned by 996 AD, making this one of the earliest recorded localities in Poland. Cracow had a bishopric from the year 1000, the town having taken shape around the defensive settlement on the Wawel Hill originating in prehistory. Cracow was in fact a Czech town in the 10th century, becoming Polish from 990 onwards. It became Polish capital in the days of Kazimierz I "the Restorer" (reigning 1034-1058), and when the country was fragmented post-1138, it was acknowledged that the Prince reigning in Cracow had ultimate control over all Polish lands. The city's capacity to do that was gravely compromised in 1241, however, a Tartar invasion bringing such ruination that the events are recalled to this day – via the now-comical *lajkonik* (whose costume depicts a mounted Tartar warrior), as well as the *hejnał* bugle-call sounded from the tower of St. Mary's Church. The rebuilt city enjoyed the right to govern itself (from 1257),

and the rule from Cracow beginning in 1306 ushered in still-greater significance, in that Prince Władysław "the Short" had himself crowned King of all Poland in the Wawel Cathedral in 1320. His successor Kazimierz the Great founded the **Cracow Academy – Poland's first university**, in 1364. Mediaeval Cracow was a Hanseatic town, as well as a centre of the Gothic style whose influence extended across Poland. From the late 15th century, this was also the headquarters of Polish printing and publishing. There were 20,000 people here by the 16th century, though capital-city status was actually lost in the early 17th, notwithstanding the fact that Kings continued to be crowned here. The Swedish incursion of 1655 ushered in a dark period of no less than two centuries of invasions, fires, epidemics and bloodily-repressed insurrections. For reasons beyond its control, Cracow's allegiances were to change five times: seized by Prussia in 1794, it transferred to Austria the next year. It fell within the Duchy of Warsaw from 1809, but was a Free City between 1815 and 1846. It then went back to Austria, allowing things to take a somewhat more favourable turn, with the population growing and industry flourishing. The **railway line to Silesia** was completed in 1844. As Austria metamorphosed into the Austro-Hungarian Empire, Cracow post-1867 became more recognisably a centre for Polish artistic, scientific and political life (even if the country itself

Illustration from *The Chronicle* by H. Schedl, published in Nuremberg in 1493, presenting **Cracow at the foot of the Wawel** surrounded by walls, a similarly fortified **Kazimierz** behind the old course of the Vistula, and **Kleparz,** a suburb of Cracow at the time.

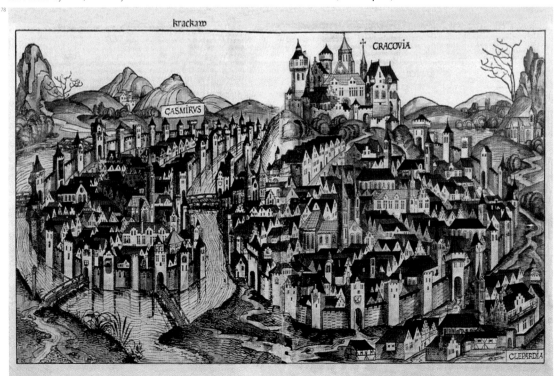

Lajkonik – a mason master dressed as a Tartar horseman parading through the streets of Cracow, commemorating the city's resistance against the Tartars, who were driven back with the help of the Vistula rafters.

Members of **the Longbow Brotherhood** cultivate shooting traditions, and during public celebrations they parade in historical dress.

remained off the map). Polish-own armed forces were set up here during World War I, helping the country to independence. Alas, the Nazi Occupation began harshly enough in Cracow, 184 professors and scientific personnel of the Jagiellonian University being rounded up and sent to the Sachsenhausen concentration camp (a number were murdered). The Wawel Castle became the seat of a merciless Governor-General, on whose orders Cracow's 68,000 Jews were first confined to a Ghetto, and then exterminated. On the eve of their expulsion by Soviet forces, the Occupants set about dynamiting Cracow's great buildings, fortunately being thwarted in their efforts by the resistance movement. After the War, Cracovians proved less than enthusiastic about the new communist masters, taking part in large-scale displays of Polish patriotism on May 3rd 1946, for example. The powers-that-be thus decided to treat this bourgeois society to an "injection of proletarian blood", this bearing fruit in the mammoth

A fireman trumpeter playing **the *hejnał* bugle call** from a high window in the tower of Mariacki (St. Mary's) Church.

View from the tower of the Mariacki Church towards **Wawel Royal Castle**.

Kurza Stopka **(Hen's Foot)** tower – a remaining element of the Gothic Castle of the Piast Family with the pavilion of Władysław Jagiełło; behind the Renaissance part of the castle built in the years 1502-1529, and the baroque helmet of the tower dating from the 17th century.

Wawel hill by the Vistula river is the oldest settled place in Cracow; in the foreground **the Royal Castle**, behind **the Cathedral**.

Pope John Paul II in the window of the Cracow archiepiscopal palace on a visit to his homeland in 2002 year.

Nowa Huta steelworks and workers' residential district. Hardly cutting-edge technology even at the time, the works produced such pollution and acid rain that much damage to (old) Cracow's architectural heritage was done. Nevertheless, things began to look up, particularly from 1978, when Archbishop of Cracow **Karol Wojtyła** became Pope John Paul II, while the city's heritage buildings found a place on **the UNESCO list of World Heritage Sites**. In detail, the listed complex comprises the **Wawel Cathedral** (11th-18th c.), with its 16th-century **Zygmuntowska Chapel,** and the **Royal Castle** (14th-20th c.), along with the **Mediaeval town layout with Market Square** and **remains of the old fortifications** (the Barbican and parts of the old walls including the Florian Gate and *Planty* park), churches representative of styles from the Romanesque

Celebrations in honour of St. Stanislaw – May 8th of each year bring crowds of the faithful to the Church on the Rock. This celebration dates back to the 11th century.

The Confession of St. Stanislaw in Wawel Cathedral;
a silver sarcophagus made by Gdańsk goldsmith, Peter van Rennen,
between the years 1669-1671.

The Wawel Cathedral – its highest tower, the Clock Tower,
is crowned with a helmet designed by Kasper Bażanka in 1716;
at the foot of the Silver Bells Tower you can see a Romanesque
fortified wall dating from before 1088.

The Romanesque towers of **St. Andrew's Church**
crowned with baroque helmets. In the background
the Jesuit church of St. Peter and St. Paul.

(e.g. **St. Andrew's**), via the Gothic (e.g. the 14th-
and 15th-century **St. Mary's**), through to the Baroque
(e.g. **St. Ann's**), and secular buildings like the
14th-16th century **Cloth Hall** and the University's
Collegium Maius (15th-16th c.). There are also the **Jewish
architectural heritage of Kazimierz**, not to mention
Cracow's old tenement houses, aristocratic mansions,
and public buildings like the **Słowacki Theatre** and
Old Theatre (*Stary Teatr*). There are also numerous
Secessionist-style examples, together with other
representative 19th- and early 20th-century buildings.

Stained glass window presenting *God the Creator*, executed by
Stanisław Wyspiański in 1900 for the Franciscan Church,
whose origins date back to 1237-1269.

In 1401 King Władysław Jagiello funded the building
of **the Collegium Maius**, the historical seat of the university college.

Floriańska Street – the first stretch of road in Cracow that the newly elected kings took on their coronation parade to Wawel Cathedral.

Relics of the northern segment of the fortified walls of Cracow with **the Florian Gate dating from** before 1307, and the Pasamonik tower dating from the end of the 15th century, which can be seen further on.

The Sukiennice (Cloth Hall) stands in the center of the Main Market Square and was constructed by the placing of a roof over the two rows of medieval stalls.

The interior of The Basilica of the Virgin Mary [The Mariacki Church] – a wooden crucifix dating from 1490, and in the chancel the large Gothic altarpiece carved by Veit Stoss (in Poland also known as Wit Stwosz).

The Mariacki Church as seen from the Main Market Square. Every hour on the hour a trumpeter plays the hejnał bugle call to the four directions of the world from its high tower.

The interior of the **Juliusz Słowacki Theatre**. This fine building, modeled on the Paris Opera House, was built between the years 1888-1893 to the design of Jan Zawiejski.

The Old Theatre on Szczepański Square. Helena Modrzejewska (Modjeska) performed here at the beginning of what would prove to be an illustrious international career.

Initially **the Old Synagogue** in Cracow's Kazimierz was a Gothic building, whereas in 1570 it was rebuilt in the Renaissance style by Mateusz Gucci. Today it houses a Jewish Museum, which is a section of the Historical Museum of the City of Cracow.

The abandoned **hall of the Sendzimir Steelworks (previously the Lenin Steelworks)** in the 1990s, following the political transformation from a communist to market economy.

The Panorama of Nowa Huta (New Steelworks). Nowa Huta saw dynamic development in the 1950s and 60s. The steelworks belching smoke into the sky on the horizon bore the name of Lenin during this time.

5. Wielkopolska as cradle of Poland

The name **Wielkopolska** literally means Great Poland, but above all denotes Old Poland, since it was here – in the pre-Christian era of the 7th century – that the **Polanian tribes** who gave a beginning to Poland came into existence. Polanian means "field-dwellers", and reflects the fact that this group of Western Slavs was quick to take up agriculture, rural crafts and commerce. It is with their tribal lands that we find the oldest Polish stories and legends linked. Lech the Pole is said to have been joined by his brothers Czech and Rus in coming out of the Pannonian region (coinciding with the area today extending from western Hungary to Bosnia and doubtless reflecting a genuine out-migration of peoples during the Dark Ages). The white eagle that came to symbolise Poland bred at the "settlement around the nest", i.e. *Gniezdno* in Polish, this name later becoming corrupted into **Gniezno**, which was Poland's first capital. Not far away is Kruszwica, in whose tower the evil King Popiel ended up being consumed by mice!

In fact, the Polanians were not the first to occupy this land, as archaeological findings in **Biskupin**, and more recently in Bruszczewo, make clear. Wielkopolska is also home to the city of **Kalisz**, which is linked with the *Kalisia* referred to by Ptolemy. Beyond their original Gniezdno and Giecz,

the Polanians gradually came to attach political importance to the **Ostrów Lednicki settlement**, the place that is associated with Poland's "baptism" (**acceptance of Christianity**) in **966**.

Today, as for many centuries, the key centre in Wielkopolska is the city of **Poznań**, situated on the River Warta, and developed out of the defensive settlement associated with the first ruler of Poland, Mieszko I, as well as the country's first religious leader, Bishop Jordan, whose seat this was from the year 968 onwards. Town rights were first conferred between 1231 and 1253, and this has long remained the capital of the region, notwithstanding competition from Gniezno, Kalisz or Szamotuły.

Today's Poznań is a city of nearly 600,000 inhabitants, an important industrial, cultural and scientific centre, and above all a place to do business. The International Poznań Fairs have been held here since 1925, and even before that there was a 19th-century flourishing of industry and agriculture that left this region as the most economically advanced part of what is today Poland (back then that name was simply absent from the map of Europe). To this day the region's inhabitants stand out for their entrepreneurship, respect for the law and effectiveness of action. It was also right here in 1918 that Poland's most

Biskupin – the reconstructed part of a **stronghold from the Lusatian period**.
In 1933 a local teacher discovered the relics of the fortified settlement dating to around 550 BC.

102

Giecz Grodziszczko excavation findings from an early Polish stronghold are on display in the museum pavilion of the **archaeological reserve**.

Konin – a sandstone post – the oldest Polish road sign, which was erected in 1151 halfway between Kruszwica and Kalisz), at present by the Church of St Bartholomew.

successful ever national uprising took place, ensuring that Wielkopolska would become part of the Polish state at that moment re-emerging after more than a century of partitioned non-existence. Attempts to Germanise the region during the War years failed, despite mass expulsions of the Polish population (involving 100,000 inhabitants of Poznań alone). Likewise, a workers' revolt in Poznań in June 1956 shook the communist state to its foundations and initiated political change. Tourists are drawn to this region by the historic buildings of Poznań, Gniezno and Kalisz. **Poznań Parish Church** is one of Poland's most beautiful Baroque-style places

Ostrów Lednicki – ruins of an early-Romanesque **palatium** dating from the 10th century.

The Międzyrzec Fortified Region – fortifications from the first half of the 20th century. The photograph shows anti-tank obstacles – the "teeth of the dragon".

Kalisz: collegiate church of the Assumption of the Virgin Mary with the sanctuary of St Joseph.

A girl in **Bamberg traditional dress**. The Poznań Bamberg Society continues to cultivate the customs and folklore of the Bamberg settlers, who came to Poznań in the 18th century.

A piper – the art of the playing the windpipe in Wielkopolska continues to be handed down from generation to generation.

of worship, while the **Town Hall** (whose tower features butting mechanical goats) is one of the finest items of secular Renaissance architecture anywhere north of the Alps. The city has a noble theatrical tradition, so it is worth being here for the *Malta* theatrical festival in early summer. There is also a famous choir from here, and music and dance ensembles. **Gniezno Cathedral** is Poland's oldest, and has many priceless items of religious art, while other fine heritage buildings include the **Castle in Szamotuły**, the **palaces in Rydzyna and Śmielów**, and the park-palace complexes in **Kórnik**, **Rogalin and Gołuchów**. The region's rich history is also attested

Poznań – the interior of **St Stanisław's Parish Church**. Design plans of the church, built between the years 1651-1653 by the Jesuits, were sent from Rome.

Following a fire in 1536 that completely destroyed **Poznań's Town Hall**, Italian architect Giovanni Battista Quadro was commissioned to oversee the reconstruction of the building, which took place in the years 1550-1560, whereby a Renaissance loggia and attic were added.

Poznań – the Gothic **Cathedral of Saint Peter and Paul** in Ostów Tumski was erected on the remains of a Romanesque church dating from the 10th century.

The interior of one of the exhibition halls at **the Poznań International Fair**.

to by monumental churches and monasteries scattered across it, e.g. at Strzelno, Mogilno and Gostyń.
And set among the picturesque lakes are **racing stables** at Racot and Golejewek. Finally, the beautiful **Wielkopolski National Park** established in 1957 protects unique post-glacial landforms, and boasts numerous lakes and patches of old forest.

Gniezno – a **Gothic crucifix** from the collection of the Cathedral Treasury can be viewed in the Museum of the Gniezno Archdiocese.

The Gniezno Doors are a pair of winged bronze doors dating from the 12th century which feature 18 panels, each masterfully engraved with a different scene from the life of St Wojciech.

Confessions over the Tomb of St Wojciech's in Gniezno Cathedral. The silver coffin carved by Peter van der Rennen in 1662, was partially reconstructed after having been mindlessly pillaged in 1986.

The Cathedral of the Assumption of the Virgin Mary in Gniezno is a religious sanctuary as well as a treasury of national relics. It was built in the 14th century on the remains of a Romanesque church, which in turn had been built on the site of a pagan temple dating from the 8th century.

The hunting lodge of Antoni Radziwiłł in Antonin with its wooden 3-storey open interior designed by Karl Friedrich Schinkel.

The castle of Izabela Działyńska (née Czartoryska) in Gołuchów is one of the most exquisite examples of the French Renaissance in Poland.

The castle of Tytus Działyński in Kórnik, converted in the 19th century from its Gothic origins. The castle holds the collection of the Kórnik Polish Academy of Sciences Library and boasts an array of treasures and curios.

The Baroque **palace of the Leszczyński Family in Rydzyna** was built between the years 1685-1695 from the reconstruction of a knight's castle dating to the early 15th century. Between the years 1705-1709 it was the residence of the Polish king, Stanisław Leszczyński.

Study of **the Raczyński Family Palace in Rogalin**. The palace, built in the 18th century, was designed with the participation of royal architects Domenico Merlini and Jan Christian Kamsetzer.

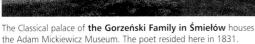

The Classical palace of **the Gorzeński Family in Śmiełów** houses the Adam Mickiewicz Museum. The poet resided here in 1831.

This eighteenth-century **manor house** was preserved **in Koszuty** near Środa Wielkopolska – today it houses the Museum of the Środa Region.

The interior of **the small chamber in the inn** is an element of the exhibition of the Wielkolpolski Ethnographic Park in **Dziekanowice**.

The late Baroque dome (1781) of **the church in Trzemeszno**. This church was built on the site of an early 12th century Romanesque basilica, within the grounds of an abbey established in the 10th century.

The Bernardine Abbey in Mogilno,
in north-eastern Wielkopolska, was established
in the 11th century and is one of the oldest abbeys in Poland.

128
129
130
131
132

Baroque altar in the Bernardine **church of Sieraków**, funded by Piotr Opaliński.

Former monastic **church** of the Cistercian nuns **in Ołobok**, south of Kalisz.

The Sanctuary of Our Lady of Licheń is the largest Catholic Church in Poland, built between the years 1994-2004; its architect was Barbara Bielecka.

Verdant oak forest situated within the boundaries of **the Wielkopolski National Park**.

The lake on the Merześnica River has proven to be a popular tourist attraction. The highest mountain in the Ostrzeszowskie Hills is Kobyla Góra (Mare's Mountain), rising to 284 m asl.

In the south-west part of Wielkopolska **the members of folk ensemble "Sieradzanie"** continue to follow folk art and cultural traditions.

In the 19th century Wielkopolska and Silesia had the densest rail grid in Poland. Today vintage steam engines travel on tourist routes. Here the photograph presents **the Szreniawa train station** on the route from Poznań to Wolsztyn.

Crop circles of unknown origin in Wylatowo – although many suspect the work of UFOs. The name of this town stems from the verb "to flyaway".

The Racot stud stable specializes in the breeding of pedigree half-breed horses with horses of the Wielkopolska region. This breed can be used for horseback riding and horse-carts, as well as for sports and recreation.

6. Selected portraits of Polish kings

The pagan Dukes of the Piast family heading the state of the Polanians are known only by their names, like Siemowit, Leszek and Siemomysł. However, from the year 960 onwards, the country came under the rule of the better-known **Mieszko I**, who became a Christian in 966. It was his son **Bolesław the Brave** who received a royal crown from Holy Roman Emperor Otto III in the year 1000. His formal coronation did not take place until 1025, however. Mieszko II never gained the crown: following wars and pagan rebellions the state simply ceased to exist. The country was rebuilt by **Kazimierz "the Restorer"** (reigning 1034-1058), his successors being **Bolesław II "the Bold"**, **Władysław** (Włodzisław) **Herman** and **Bolesław III "the Wrymouth"**. The latter, wishing to spare his sons any battle over who would inherit, established a principle that the oldest son would rule over the whole of Poland, while his younger siblings would rule in given provinces only. Alas, the brothers started warring in spite of everything, and the senior one, Władysław II, actually left the country in 1146, hence his status as "the Exile". That left, as successive occupiers of the throne: **Bolesław "the Curly"**, **Mieszko "the Old"** and **Kazimierz "the Just"**. After 1195, the country finally splintered into separate Piast dukedoms. In 1290, Cracow was taken by the Czech King Wacław, while 1295 brought the coronation of Przemysł II in Wielkopolska. His inheritor was King **Władysław "the Short"**, who ascended the throne after years of fighting, bringing a return to rule by the Piasts. Władysław's son **Kazimierz the Great** strengthened the country, brought order to the legal system, entered into beneficial alliances, fortified the realm and founded Poland's first university in 1364. His nephew and successor **King Louis of Hungary** made a start to the Angevin Dynasty in Poland (in 1370), though this ended with his daughter Jadwiga, who ruled in her own right between 1384 and 1399, seeing to it that there was peace wherever possible, but also knowing how to stand up for Polish interests when necessary. She ultimately married **Duke Jagiełło of Lithuania**, whose baptismal name was Władysław. Jadwiga was already a prospect for sainthood at the time of her death. Jagiełło gained the right to inherit for his descendents and grew famous for his victory at the Battle of Grunwald in 1410. Implementing Jadwiga's last wishes, the King supported the University in Cracow, which became known henceforth as the Jagiellonian. The oldest of his sons, **Władysław of Varna**, was King of both Poland (1434-1444) and Hungary (1440-1444), while his younger son **Kazimierz Jagiellon** was Grand Duke of Lithuania, as well as King of Poland up to 1492. Through this personal union with Lithuania, Poland became a political force to be reckoned with, enjoying access to both the Baltic and Black Seas. It was during the times of King **Jan Olbracht** and **Aleksander Jagiellon** that the uniquely Polish system of the democracy of the nobility took shape, while the reign of the latter's successor – **Zygmunt I** – was very much a golden age from the point

A Byzantine-styled monument of **Mieszko I** and **Bolesław Chrobry** in the Golden Chapel of Poznań Cathedral executed in the years 1834-1837.

Gravestone of **Kazimierz Wielki** (Kazimierz the Great) in Wawel Cathedral, executed in the years 1370-1382.

BOLESLAUS CHRABRY

VENCESLAUS BOHEMUS

VLADISLAUS LOCTIUS

CASIMIRUS MAGNUS

In the golden-framed portraits by Marcello Bacciarelli (1731-1818) the kings of Poland are introduced: **Bolesław Chrobry** (967-1025), the founder of the sovereign state; **Wacław of Czech** (1271-1305), a gifted reformer; **Władysław Łokietek** (1260-1333) an indefatigable warrior; **Kazimierz the Great** (1310-1370) an outstanding politician, and the founder of the Academy of Cracow; **Ludwik (Louis) of Hungary** (1326-1382) a giver of privileges; **Władysław Jagiełło** (1348-1434) Ludwik's son-in-law, a Lithuanian, and the founder of the Jagiellonian dynasty; **saint Jadwiga** (1374-1399), stateswoman; **Władysław Warneńczyk** (1424-1444), a tragic hero; **Kazimierz Jagiellończyk** (1427-1492), who strengthened the power-base of the Jagiellonian dynasty.

LUDOVICUS HUNGARUS

VLADISLAUS JAGIELLO

of view of Polish culture. King **Zygmunt II August**, another patron of the arts and collector of masterpieces, worked to strengthen the Polish-Lithuanian union, this bearing fruit in the appearance of the Commonwealth of the Two Nations in 1569. Following his death, all further monarchs were identified and chosen by means of election. In 1573, **Henri of Valois** took the reins, only to leave to ascend the French throne a year later. The King (literally) from 1575 was **Anna Jagiellonka**, who married the Duke of Somlyo **Stefan Batory**, who then became king. His reign (from 1576-1586) marked the peak of the country's military achievements, and was also a time of order at home. Thus powerful at the moment of his election in 1587, **Zygmunt III Waza** sought the throne of Sweden and thereby launched into a war that would last 66 years. He was unable to keep the peace with Turkey (suffering a major military setback at the Battle of Cecora in 1620), while the conflict with Moscow he engendered continues to have its consequences in our own 21st-century times. Elected in 1632, King Zygmunt's son **Władysław IV** tried to bring the Cossacks into the fold, but instead encouraged them to lead Ukraine into a bloody war with Poland itself. Władysław's brother – the third monarch of the Waza Dynasty, **Jan Kazimierz**, would ultimately renounce any claim to the throne of Sweden, but would in the meantime bring Poland destruction and a decline in significance. An unsuccessful attempt at reform led to his forced abdication in 1668. **Michał Korybut-Wiśniowiecki** ruled for just 4 years. The triumph of his successor, **Jan III Sobieski,** at the 1683 Battle of Vienna in essence put an end to conflicts with the Turks, though it actually saved the bacon of Poland's enemy Austria. The ambitious **August II of Saxony** began his reign with a victory over the Tartars (in what would turn out to be the last war won by the Polish side until 1918), ending it on a lower note

HEDVIGIS

VLADISLAUS VARNENSIS

CASIMIRUS JAGIELLONIDES

IOHANNES ALBERTUS

SIGISMUNDUS I

SIGISMUNDUS AUGUSTUS

HENRICUS VALESIUS

Jan Olbracht (1459-1501), the grandson of Jagiełło;
Zygmunt I Stary ("the Old") (1467-1548), who presided over
the golden age of Polish culture; **Zygmunt II August** (1520-1572)
patron of the arts, and guardian of religious tolerance;
Barbara Radziwiłłówna (1520-1551), the love of Zygmunt August,
married in 1547, without the knowledge of the ruling Zygmunt Stary
– portrait from the Front Entrance Hall of the Royal Castle in Warsaw.

Anna Jagiellonka (1523-1596), the last member of the dynasty
– *Portrait in a Widow's Dress* by Marcin Kober (not-signed).

Henryk Walezy (Henri of Valois) (1551-1589),
introduced the fashion of eating with a fork.

with his 1706 abdication. From 1704, the crown had passed
to **Stanisław Leszczyński,** whose election was very much
the achievement of Swedish force of arms. August returned
to power in 1709 thanks to the Russians. After his death
(in 1733), Leszczyński returned as King in the wake
of the last truly free election. He forsook his coronation
and shot off to Gdańsk in search of the funding that would
support further war. In the meantime, the Russians
in Warsaw had made sure that **August III of Saxony** was
chosen as King, his coronation taking place in Cracow
in 1734. Last King of Poland **Stanisław August
Poniatowski** made a valiant if doomed effort to free
Poland of its Russian yoke. His abdication in 1795 coincided
with nothing less than Poland's disappearance from
the map of Europe. Under Polish law, the title of King was
also rightfully borne by Fryderyk August, Duke of Warsaw
in the years 1807-1815, as well as by the Tsars crowned
in Warsaw and known as Aleksander Pawłowicz (1815)
and Mikołaj I (1825).
The best-known likenesses of Polish kings were those
created by Italian painter Marcello Bacciarelli on commission
from King Stanisław August Poniatowski in the late 18th
century. The 22 oils can be seen today in the Marble Room
of Warsaw's Royal Castle. Then there was Jan Matejko,
whose work of the years 1890-1892 comprised 44 pencil
sketches now so well-known to Poles that they are
subconsciously considered to represent actual likenesses
of the monarchs portrayed.

STEPHANUS BATOREUS

SIGISMUNDUS III

The Column of **Zygmunt III Waza** on Castle Square in Warsaw.

Stefan Batory (1533-1586), a great leader,
a true monarch; **Zygmunt III Waza** (1566-1632),
in 1620 he survived an attempt on his life.

38

VLADISLAUS QUARTUS

IOANNUS CASIMIRUS

MICHAEL I

IOHANNES TERTIUS

Władysław IV Waza (1595-1648), who established Poland's naval fleet; **Jan Kazimierz** (1609-1672) allowed his wife, Maria Ludwika Gonzaga, to initiate the publishing of the first Polish newspaper, which in 1661 appeared as *The Polish Mercury*; **Michał Korybut Wiśniowiecki** (1638-1673), a polyglot; **Jan III Sobieski** (1624-1696), the defender of Europe, the last sovereign monarch of Poland.

Marcello Baciarelli's *The Relief of Vienna* – equestrian portrait of **Jan III Sobieski** - one of the six images of the *History of Poland and Lithuania* cycle, located in the Knight's Room of the Royal Castle in Warsaw.

August II of Saxony (1670-1733), called "The Strong" by virtue of his ability to bend horseshoes with his bare hands; **August III of Saxony** (1696-1763), thanks to his passivity and helplessness he was remembered by his subjects as a "good master"; **Stanisław August Poniatowski** (1732-1798), in his coronation dress, a patron of the arts and sciences. He was the patron of Marcello Baciarelli, the painter of this portrait.

STANISLAUS AUGUSTUS

AUGUSTUS II

AUGUSTUS III

7. The larger cities...

Of the 41 Polish cities with over 100,000 inhabitants, 12 are located in Upper Silesia. Among them, **Katowice** (with 334,000 people) is the product of the 19th-century Industrial Revolution. The Silesian Museum here has a leading collection of Polish art dating from the years 1800-1939, while the University of Silesia boasts one of Poland's most modern libraries. A still-newer library graces the University in **Łódź**, a centrally-located city of 778,000 inhabitants. This grew up as a major textile centre employing people of many ethnic origins, notably Poles, Germans, Jews and Russians. Today it has as many as 20 academic institutions, among which a key player is the Film School that trained Polish greats Roman Polański, Andrzej Wajda and Krzysztof Kieślowski. Among other attractions are the mansions of the old industrialists, souvenirs of the life of Artur Rubinstein, and Poland's number-one collection of 20th-century art (with work by Strzemiński, Kobro, Hiller and Witkacy). The old factories have now been made over into shopping and entertainment centres, apartment blocks and cultural venues, but origins are still recalled in the "Dialogue between Four Cultures" Festival. **Wrocław** (632,000 people) is on the River Oder (Odra in Polish). This was a fortified settlement of the *Ślężanie* from the 7th century, though the first traces of settlement go back further, in association with the trade routes for Baltic amber.

A Polish bishopric was established here in the year 1000, though town rights were only conferred by the Silesian Piasts in 1214. This was a Czech town from 1335, in Prussia from 1742 and reincorporated into Poland in 1945, if as little more than a smoking ruin. Solidarity operated underground here between 1981 and 1989, while massive flooding afflicted the city in 1997. On a happier note, 2002 brought the 300th anniversary of the founding of Wrocław University. Today's Wrocław recalls, not only its own heritage, but also that of the once-Polish city of Lwów (now Ukrainian Lviv), from which such important institutions as the Ossolineum and the Technical University were transferred in the post-War period. **Gdańsk** (457,000 people) received its charter in the 13th century, having previously been a fortified settlement overlooking the port on the Motława. St. Adalbert came here in 997, while less welcome visitors were the Teutonic Knights, who took over in 1308, and only left in 1454. Nevertheless, this was both the largest and the wealthiest city in Poland from the 15th century on, passing to Prussia in 1793, though being under Napoleon's rule in the years 1807-1815. The special status of Free City applied between 1920 and 1939, when Hitler incorporated it into the Third Reich. The Red Army saw to it that the city's 1945 liberation from Nazi rule also entailed its incineration,

Cities such as Katowice or Łódź enjoyed the benefits of the Industrial Revolution in the 19th century, and today they are homes to many fine examples of industrial architecture – both factory and residential. The photograph shows **Nikiszowiec – a district of Katowice**.

165

Building of the Silesian Museum on Korfanty Avenue **in Katowice**. It was established in 1929 as a symbol of Silesian Polishness. It was destroyed in World War II and only reopened in 1984.

the "old" Gdańsk we see today being a reconstruction. The city's new housing estates were the cradle of 1970s workers protests that gave rise to *Solidarność* in 1980. Pope John Paul II came here in 1987, meeting Solidarity hero and Nobel Prizewinner Lech Wałęsa. Gdańsk's other Nobel winner (for Literature) is Günter Grass. The port city of **Szczecin** (with 416,000 inhabitants) was a Slav mercantile state with its own laws from the 9th century on. It accepted Christianity in 1124. It was the capital of the Duchy of Pomerania until 1637, when it fell to the Swedes. It then passed to the Prussians after 1720, only coming back to Poland in 1945. There were popular uprisings here in 1970 and 1980, while the city of Szczecin in a free Poland played host to the Tall Ships in 2007. **Lublin** – a town established in 1317 now comprising 354,000 people – is the seat of two important places of learning: the Catholic University of Lublin and Maria Skłodowska-Curie University. It was in Lublin that

Katowice's Spodek (Saucer) hall, hosting sports events, concerts and fairs, was built in 1971 to the design of Maciej Gintowt and Maciej Krasiński. Andrzej Żórawski was the chief engineer.

Exhibition in **the Central Textile Industry Museum in Łódź** – antique weaving machine in the White Factory Hall of Ludwik Geyer.

Artur Rubinstein's (1887-1982) **Monument** on Piotrkowska Street **in Łódź**, in the background a group portrait of eminent citizens of Łódź on the wall of a 19th century tenement.

Israel Kalmanowicz Poznański owned the second largest cotton factory **in Łódź**, whereas the **dining room** in his **palace**, built between the years 1890-1903 to the design of Hilary Majewski and Adolf Seligson, is one of the most opulent interiors in the city.

the 1569 Act of Union between Poland and Lithuania creating the Commonwealth of the Two Nations was concluded. In consequence, a royal tribunal was located here from 1578. This was long a great Jewish community, hence the convening here in 1623 of the Sejm of Jews of the Polish Crown, as well as the presence in the city of institutions training Rabbis. The Nazi response was that place of Jewish martyrdom and suffering, the Majdanek Extermination Camp, as well as a prison in the castle from which the NKVD supplanted the Gestapo in 1944. **Częstochowa** (252,000 people) is an industrial and academic centre, as well as a major place of pilgrimage associated with the cult of the Virgin Mary. The monastery at Jasna Góra draws over 6 million pilgrims

The Old Town Hall on the Podzamcze **in Szczecin** was erected in the 13th century, and rebuilt in the 17th century. It was destroyed in 1945 and rebuilt once more after the war, when it became the seat of Szczecin Museum.

Szczecin – view of the Chrobry Embankments, a complex of fine buildings in the Vilhelmian Baroque style, built on the terrace of the Odra river valley between the years 1902-1921. Moored boats participated in **The Tall Ships Races** in August, 2007.

Wing of **the Castle of the Pomeranian Princes in Szczecin**. Almost completely destroyed between the years 1942-1944 in British and American air raids on the port and the nearby weapons factory, the castle, was rebuilt in a Renaissance style.

Endowed by Jagiełło in 1418, the Gothic palm ceiling and walls of **the Castle Chapel in Lublin** are adorned by Byzantine-Russian paintings featuring scenes from The Passion and Old and New Testament scenes, attributed to Master Andrzej and other painters of Ruś Halicko-Włodzimierska. It is an example of the mutual enrichment of both Western and Eastern European cultures.

The beginnings of **Lublin Castle** are associated with the Halitian prince, Leo Daniłowicz, who occupied Lublin in 1280; Kazimierz Wielki fortified the city in the middle of the 14th century, and during this time the Gothic royal castle was also built, later to be rebuilt in the neo-Gothic style between the years 1824-1826.

a year. **Toruń** (206,000 people) was a Hanseatic city in the Middle Ages, growing rich through the trade in cereals along the River Vistula. Peace treaties with the Teutonic Knights were signed here in 1411 and 1466. The tradition in astronomy began with the birth of Copernicus in the city in 1473, while the Department of Radio Astronomy at the University employs its former graduate Aleksander Wolszczan, discoverer of the first extra-solar planetary system in 1991. A modern planetarium was founded in Toruń in 1994. Another Vistula-side locality with a picturesque location is **Płock**, one of the smaller of Poland's cities, with 127,000 inhabitants. It played an important historical role as capital of Mazovia, the seat of a bishop from 1075, and capital of all Poland between 1079 and 1138. Today it plays host to the largest petrochemical works in the country.

Lublin – view of the Gothic-Renaissance tower of **the Cracow Gate** (1525), the classical **Town Hall** (1828), and the residential **Krakowskie Przedmieście Street**.

The Baroque **Leopoldin Lecture Hall** built in 1732 to the design by Franz Joseph Mangoldt and Johann Christoph Handke, as part of a **complex of buildings that made up Wrocław University.**

Interior of **the Church of the Blessed Virgin Mary on Piasek Island ("piasek" meaning sand), which** is a big island in the Odra River, one of earliest settled places in the **Wrocław area.**

Wrocław – St John the Baptist Cathedral as seen from the Tumski Bridge. The city is often covered in fog as it is situated on a network of rivers and canals.

View in the direction of **Wrocław Market Square** from the tower of St Elizabeth's church.

The Imperial Bridge **in Wrocław,** opened in 1910 in the presence of the emperor Wilhelm II. Destroyed in World War II, it was later rebuilt as **Grunwald Bridge.** In the background, on Grunwald Square are residential houses with exquisite facades and cramped interiors.

Baroque stairs in the large entrance hall
of **the Main Town Hall in Gdańsk**.

Church of the Blessed Virgin Mary in Gdańsk, interior of the
largest Gothic church in Poland. Master Paweł sculpted the crucifixion
scene on a rainbow beam around the year 1517. In the foreground
a Renaissance baptistery with a Baroque baptismal font and
personifications of the virtues.

Excursion boats along **Long Embankment in Gdańsk**. The silhouette
of the Crane – the port lift dating from the 15th century,
reflected in the waters of the Old Motława river.

The silhouette of the Church of the Blessed Virgin Mary
and the Town Hall tower with the golden figure of Zygmunt August
on the spire dominating the rooftop panorama **Main City of Gdańsk**.

Neptune's Fountain in Gdańsk's Long Market,
built in the 17th century. According to sailor folklore, the famous
Gdańsk Goldwasser vodka would gush from this fountain.

According to tradition, **the image of the Black Madonna of Jasna Góra** was painted by St Luke the Evangelist. It was offered to the Jasna Góra monastery by its founder, prince Władysław Opolczyk in 1382.

Fortified complex of the Pauline Monastery in **Jasna Góra in Częstochowa** – an annual pilgrimage destination for millions of Catholics from all over the world.

Częstochowa – the gathering of pilgrims praying at the walls of the Jasna Góra Monastery. The first mass group of pilgrims arrived here from Warsaw in 1711.

Road bridge across **the Vistula in Toruń** and the riverside **part of the Old Town** as seen from the tower of St John's Church.

Toruń, the baroque pulpit in the Gothic **Church of St John the Baptist and St John the Evangelist**. The vaulting dome and elements of the medieval polychrome date from around 1338.

Statue of the most famous citizen of Toruń, **Nicolas Copernicus**, the author of the heliocentric model of the Universe, is situated in the square in front of **Toruń Town Hall**.

The Classicist **Town Hall in Płock**, built with great panache between the years 1824-1849.

The Renaissance **Cathedral in Płock,** built on the remains of its Romanesque predecessor from the 12th century, rebuilt between the years 1532-1535 and 1556-1563 with the participation of Italian architects working in Poland.

The Mazovian Museum **in Płock** prides itself on having the best **Art Nouveau collection** in Poland.

8. ...and smaller cities and towns

Away from Upper Silesia and the coastal Tri-City region, Poland's larger cities tend to be rather regularly distributed across the country and are mostly not critical in shaping its landscape. In some contrast, the smaller cities and larger towns may at times stun us with the richness of their history and exceptional monuments. Many retain their original layouts from the Middle Ages, with a centrally-located main market square that attests to a commercial genesis. Exemplary in this respect is **Sandomierz** – one of the country's oldest towns, resided in continuously since the 8th century and granted town rights from 1227. An important regional centre in the past, this now has just 25,000 inhabitants. The built heritage here had a lucky escape during the Second World War, when the advancing Red Army decided against the use of artillery as it successfully crossed the River Vistula here in 1944. Further down the Vistula stands **Kazimierz Dolny**, whose name recalls Duke Kazimierz the Just. The "Dolny" part of the name (meaning "Lower") came in to distinguish the place from the "Upper" settlement located by King Kazimierz the Great and today constituting a suburb of Cracow. Up to the 17th century there was a Vistula-side port here, which grew rich along with Gdańsk and Toruń,

thanks to the trade in grain. Alas, war, plague and even changes in the course of the Vistula ensured the decline of the town, which was like an insect preserved in amber, doing nothing much until its beauty began to attract artists in the 20th century. Just as interesting a history is possessed by **Zamość** – a utopian settlement or *cita ideale* built from scratch in line with Renaissance thinking. The founder, Jan Zamoyski (1542-1605), who held the post of Crown Hetman, conferred the task of building upon Italian architect Bernardo Morando. The work on it continued from 1585 through to 1619. Today this is the world's only town with an entirely preserved layout and buildings from that era. **Zakopane** is dubbed the winter capital of Poland and, though it lacks the historical or aristocratic pedigree of other towns, it is for all that the birthplace of the *Zakopiański* style in art and architecture, devised on the basis of the Highlanders' folk styles of building and decorating by Stanisław Witkiewicz (1851-1915). Zakopane is indeed a centre for all winter sports, and a base for mountain-climbing. The summer capital of Poland would have to be **Sopot** – a seaside resort with a wooden pier that extends half a kilometre out into the Gulf of Gdańsk. It received town rights as relatively recently as in 1901,

The view from **the Market Square in Kazimierz Dolny** looking towards the parish church is a favourite subject for painters.

The Virgin Mary with Baby Jesus treading over a dragon – a fragment from the restored façade of a **tenement building in Zamość**.

The organ of the Bernardine Church in Leżajsk dates from the 17th century and is one of the oldest and most precious musical instruments in Europe.

Przemyśl is a multicultural city. Here Catholics who choose to attend the Latin mass congregate in **St. John the Baptist's Cathedral**.

The Renaissance **Town Hall on the Market Square in Sandomierz** was built around 1550 from the materials of a 14th century Gothic building.

having developed out of a place to take iodine-rich seawater established in 1823 by a doctor in Napoleon's army called Georg Haffner. Poland in fact has plenty of places – mostly small towns – supplying good mineral waters. The so-called pearl of the Polish spas is **Krynica** in the Carpathians, which has been offering hydrotherapy since 1794. The cure given here on the basis of acidic iron-rich waters may be augmented by treatment with bee products from the apiaries in Kamianna village. Among names linked with Krynica are primitivist painter Nikifor (Epifan Drowniak) and great opera singer Jan Kiepura. Other known spas include those located in the Sudety Mountains, like **Kudowa, Polanica and Lądek**, or else **Ciechocinek** in the Kujawy region where salt water has been available

The **Virgin Mary's Offertory** is the parochial church in **Wadowice** and is where Karol Wojtyła – later **Pope John Paul II** – was baptized in 1920.

Krupówki – the central street of Zakopane – a place where you can meet people from all over Poland. It is a street that has close associations with some of Poland's outstanding cultural figures of the 20th century, such as Witkacy or Władysław Hasior.

The Szczawnica spa has been offering curative treatments with its mineral waters since 1810. Local historic architecture has been preserved in an "Alpine style", typical for 19th-century mountain health resorts.

for outdoor inhalations since the 18th century. Where salt is concerned, one could do no better than **Wieliczka**, where the substance has been mined since the 13th century. The mine in existence there today is Europe's oldest in continuous operation. Its museum part, an important item of Polish heritage, extends down some 100 m below the surface. Silver mining was what made **Olkusz** rich, while some of the Silesian towns once had goldmines – now sadly worked out. Many of these were capitals of local Piast dukedoms. Thus, for example, from 1311 **Brzeg** shared this function with **Legnica** within the dukedom of Bolesław III "the Extravagant". The nickname attested indirectly to the Duke's wealth, though the greatest patron of Brzeg (who rebuilt its castle and gave it the best-stocked library in Silesia) was Bolesław's son Ludwik I. In addition, between the 17th and 20th centuries, the small towns of central and eastern Poland were very much the domain of the country's Jewish population.

The renowned **children's spa in Rabka** not only boasts rich mineral waters, but is situated in an area of pristine natural beauty. The local historic **church was built in 1606**.

Attracting the country's glitterati and literati, the beach in front of the Grand Hotel in **Sopot** was once Poland's most fashionable place to bathe.

Designed by Stanisław Staszic, the brine graduation towers and salt works of **Ciechocinek** were built in 1828 and were used for capturing salt from evaporating mineral waters.

In the 19th century on the slopes of Stożek Mountain (517 m asl) a park with a glass pavilion was built for patrons of **the Szczawno Zdrój.**

Świeradów-Zdrój. This is one of the many Lower Silesian spas known from the 16th century onwards.The photograph shows the 80 m promenade hall of the treatment centre erected in 1899.

The great Polish writer Bolesław Prus (1847-1912) was a frequent visitor to the classical palace of the Małachowskis **in Nałęczów near Lublin**, which in the 19th century was converted into a sanatorium. Today it houses a museum devoted to the writer.

Żyrardów owes its name to Filip de Girard, who invented a machine for the mechanical spinning of linen.

Historians regard cobblestones as evocative links with the past. The photograph shows **the Market Square in Pułtusk** in Mazovia.

Konstancin, situated just outside Warsaw, is a leafy town that has brine springs with curative properties. Its brine graduation tower is an open-air inhalatorium, which is said to have a positive influence on people's immune and nervous systems.

The Market Square in Cieszyn. Today 40,000 people inhabit the city. According to legend, the three brothers, Lech, Czech and Rus in 810 AD, founded Cieszyn.

Żywiec – tourists associate this town primarily with Poland's most **popular beer**. The photograph presents **the Church of the Blessed Virgin Mary's Birth**. The sepulchral chapel of the Habsburg family, the founders of the local brewery, can be found here.

In **Paczków**, at the foot of the Opawskie Mountains, there is an almost completely intact **ring of fortified walls** from the period 1341-1376.

Nysa, the portal of St. Jacob's Church. This Gothic church was built around 1430 with the assistance of "Master" Peter von Franckenstein.

Wang temple in Karpacz, in the Karkonosze Mountains, is a medieval wooden church built at the turn of the 12th and 13th centuries from the wood of Viking long boats in the town of Vang in Southern Norway. In the 19th century it was brought to Poland.

Facade of the **old Jesuit college in Legnica**. The Piast Mausoleum is located in the adjoining Church of St. John the Baptist.

Brzeg is one of the two capital cities of the medieval Brzeg-Legnica Duchy. In the photo we see **the Raising of the Holy Cross Church**, a one-nave Baroque church.

9. Polish Jews

There are Jews in Polish history as far back as it goes. Cracow was first referred to by a merchant called **Ibrahim ibn Jakub**, who ventured into central Europe in the 10th century. He was by then following a well-blazed trail that connected the Jews of Spain with the Khazar adherents of Judaism living by the Caspian Sea. Jewish merchants must even have settled in Poland, though early references are very few and far between. What we do know is that **more formalised Jewish communities** were already founded in **Wrocław, Przemyśl** and **Płock** by the year 1200. A little later, villages termed *Żydowo* were founded near both Gniezno and Kalisz. The first legal act addressing matters Jewish is in turn one from Wielkopolska from the year 1264. By virtue of it, Prince Bolesław the Pious sought to guarantee Jews security, freedom of conscience and the freedom to engage in trade. Rights of these kinds were extended to the whole kingdom in 1334, by King Kazimierz the Great. Not coincidentally, the 14th century brought a major influx of Jews from France and Germany. Unfortunately, the years 1349-1350 also brought an epidemic of plague for which the newcomers were blamed. However, King Kazimierz welcomed the immigrants cordially enough, settling them in a new town that he dubbed **Kazimierz**. Today this is a district of Cracow, in which it is still possible to visit many heritage buildings associated with the Jewish community once present. Furthermore, as an autonomous town through the period 1335-1796, Kazimierz was informally at least the capital for the whole Jewish diaspora in Poland. The second most important centre in the country was **Lublin** – a place of Jewish learning and philosophy from the Middle Ages through to World War II. The first **school for rabbis**, appearing here in 1518, was in receipt of a royal privilege from 1567 onwards. An edition of the *Talmud* was printed in Lublin in 1559. The city also gained the *Yeshiva Chachmei Lublin* in 1930, this being a centre of higher education for Jewish philosophers. Its founder, Jehuda Meir Szapiro (1887-1933) saw it as nothing less than the world's principal seat of rabbinic and talmudic learning. At the time, some 35% of the population of Lublin was Jewish. Post-1939, the occupying authorities from Nazi Germany set up a Ghetto here, from which residents were transported to the death camps. The establishment of ghettos cut off from the outside world was their standard practice. The **Litzmannstadt Ghetto** established in Łódź in February 1940, crammed some 160,000 people into an area of just 4 km^2. In 1941 they were joined by Jews from Austria, the Czech Republic, Luxembourg and Germany, as well as the ghettos in smaller towns in the region. These were also joined by Roma people. By 1942, the completed transfer to the death camps of the children and elderly deemed "unsuited to the production process" led to the conversion of the ghetto into a labour camp, this in turn being liquidated in August 1944. Of the 200,000 people that had been held there in total, not more than 12,000 survived the War. Most populous

A passage between tenements **in Kórnik** near Poznań, called "the eye of the needle", used to lead to the synagogue. Today it is used for storing **headstones from the now-closed Jewish cemetery**.

The Jewish cemetery in Bródno in Warsaw was established in 1784 with the permission of king Stanisław August. It was destroyed during the last war.

The house of the Süsser family on **Krakowska Street in Cracow's Kazimierz**, a view from the turn of 20th century. Jewish storehouses and shops occupied the ground floor of the tenement buildings.

Kazimierz district in Cracow. Joseph Street during the Nazi occupation in 1941.

of all was of course the **Warsaw Ghetto**, whose attempted liquidation in 1943 provoked resistance from the January onwards. In April this turned into a fully-fledged uprising, Jewish underground forces being joined by the civilian population (as supported by Home Army operations) in doing battle with German, Ukrainian and Latvian units. When these forces eventually took the ghetto, they oversaw the transfer to Treblinka of a residual population c. 60,000 strong – all that was left of the half-million people that had at one point been incarcerated within the tiny district. The fighting continued until May. While the punishment for Poles helping Jews was death, there are more individuals honoured for doing this from Poland than from any other country. Alas the copybook recounting the shared history of Polish Gentiles and Jews is severely blotted by **the events of summer 1941**. At that time there are known cases of murders being committed by Poles against their Jewish neighbours (at Jedwabne among other places). Anti-Semitic tendencies were not unknown in the country before that time, and sadly they did not disappear later either. As late as in 1945 there were **pogroms** in **Rzeszów** and **Cracow** that left 5 dead. The following year saw the most infamous event of all – costing the lives of 37

Jews had to wear armbands with the Star of David on pain of death.

Nowolipie Street in **the Warsaw ghetto**. Overcrowding meant that many Jews had to spend entire days on the street.

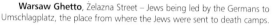

Warsaw Ghetto, Żelazna Street – Jews being led by the Germans to Umschlagplatz, the place from where the Jews were sent to death camps.

A photograph from the time of **the Warsaw Ghetto Uprising** (April-May 1943): German soldiers firing at the positions of insurgents.

One of methods used by the Nazis to fight the insurgents was to **set buildings in the ghetto on fire**. In the photograph we can see a man jumping out of the second floor window of a burning tenement.

– in **Kielce. State-sponsored Anti-Semitism by the communist authorities** got underway some 22 years later (in 1968), the support this gained among propaganda-flooded workers doing much to reinforce **the stereotype of the Anti-Semitic Pole**. Such was the virulence of the persecution that 13,000 Jews emigrated in the years 1968-1971. Present-day Poland is now witnessing concerted action to restore familiarity with the country's Jewish heritage to the collective memory. Cracow plays host to a major festival of Jewish culture. The graves of Hasidic tzadiks – spiritual leaders of a Jewish religious movement originating on Polish soil – are visited by pilgrims from Israel and the whole diaspora. Museums and other centres documenting the history of Polish Jews have also now been organised in the country's surviving synagogues.

The train station in Koło – the forced **transfer of Jews** from a passenger train to a goods train on the way to the **extermination camp in Kulmhof am Ner**.

A photograph taken by an SS guard in 1944 of **Jewish women and children in Auschwitz II-Birkenau** before entering the undressing room by gas chamber no. IV.

The Warsaw Ghetto razed to the ground, photographed in the spring of 1945.

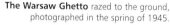

The **Museum of the History of Polish Jews POLIN** was open on April 19th 2013, marking the 70th anniversary of the start of the Uprising in the Warsaw Ghetto. The reconstructed **bema from the synagogue in Gwoździec** (now Ukrainian Hvizdets).

Monument to the Heroes of the Warsaw Ghetto on the square by Zamenhof Street, erected in 1948. It was designed by Leon Marek Suzin and sculpted by Natan Rappaport. The monument has inscriptions in three languages: Yiddish, Hebrew and Polish.

Kazimierz Dolny. The collection of stones was built from the remains of Jewish headstones in the 1980s. The crack is intended to symbolize the tragic fate of Polish Jews.

The weeping wall at the cemetery by the Remuh synagogue in Cracow.

Jedwabne – monument to the Jews murdered by Polish people in the summer of 1941.

Monument to the Memory of the Jews of Wyszków – a semi-circle wall with fragments of headstones from the old cemetery.

The Nożyks' Synagogue in Warsaw – the only synagogue to have survived World War II. The Jewish community continues to worship in the synagogue.

The interior of **the synagogue in Tykocin** from 1642, rebuilt after 1950. The center the synagogue features a Bemah on four pillars, where the Torah is read and circumcisions are carried out.

The Hanukkah lamp: eight candles lit for the eight consecutive days of the Hanukkah holiday, in commemoration of the destruction of the Jerusalem Temple – exhibit from the museum in **Kazimierz Dolny**.

A street in Cracow's Kazimierz. The district of the Remuh cemetery with reconstructed traditional signs.

A concert in Kazimierz, during a **Jewish Cultural Festival** in Cracow.

Jews praying by **the grave of rabbi Mojżesz Isserles, called Remuh**. This eminent philosopher was born and died in Cracow in the 16th century. He was the vice-chancellor of the local rabbinic college. His grave is believed to be a place of miracles. The Remuh synagogue and cemetery were so named in honour of the rabbi.

A group of **young people from Israel** at the entrance to the Remuh synagogue **in Cracow**.

The carrying of the Torah, containing the five books of Moses, during a ceremony accompanying the opening of the Hasidic synagogue **in Leżajsk**.

In March, 2008, Hasids arrived **in Leżajsk** from all over the world, on a pilgrimage to **the grave of the Tzaddik, Elimelech Weissblum**, one of the founders of the Hasidic tradition, to mark the 222nd anniversary of his death.

10. Places of oppression and murder by the Nazi German regime

In 2006, the Polish Government applied to the UNESCO Word Heritage Committee for a change of name for the remains of the camp located near Oświęcim to: "Auschwitz-Birkenau. German Nazi Concentration and Extermination Camp (1941-1945)". The application, which gained the support of the Yad Vashem Institute and the Union of Jewish Religious Communities, was received positively. It was by such precise naming that Poland sought to bring an end to the habit of referring to "Polish" death camps or extermination camps, in some Western media, whose commentators had elected to be guided by knowledge of present-day geography, rather than educating themselves as regards history in the 1939-45 era. As places designed to achieve imprisonment and oppression out of the public eye, the **Camps** were regarded by the authorities of the Third Reich as "undesirable within the German state". The idea went back as far as **1933**, the aim being the elimination of political opposition to National Socialism. However, post-1939, a switch of function ensured increasing utilisation as places in which to terrorise inmates, exploit capacities to work to and beyond the limits, and ultimately carry out their extermination – most especially if they were Jewish or from other nations or groupings deemed "inferior" by the Nazis. To ensure extermination went according to plan, death factories under SS administration were also established, as at **Kulmhof am Ner** (otherwise Chełmno nad Nerem, again in Poland). Different estimates have it that 150-315,000 people died there between 1941 and 1945. In this case, annihilation represented the last phase of a transport operation in which the exhaust-fumes of the trucks bringing those poor innocents to their place of death were directed inwards into the sealed interiors. The activity at the camp in **Treblinka**, where most of the half-million inhabitants of the Warsaw Ghetto were put to death, has been characterized as "industrial-scale genocide". Among its victims was the widely-respected pedagogue **Janusz Korczak** (Henryk Goldszmit), who refused to be parted from the orphaned children under his care, and was thus murdered alongside them at the camp. At Treblinka, the piping of combustion gases into stationary gas chambers led to the murder of some 750-800,000 people, originating in Poland, but also in many other European countries. However, an insurrection among inmates resulting in a breakout by 200 was followed by attempts to conceal this Camp's location: once the buildings had been levelled, the land was ploughed and sown with lupins. A similar situation applied at **Sobibor**, in eastern Poland, where the Nazis killed around 250,000 Jews in the years 1942-1943 – continuing until October 14th, when inmates led by Red Army prisoner Aleksander "Sacha" Pechersky managed to kill 12 SS personnel, allowing some 300 intended victims to escape. The Nazi response was again to scrupulously erase all traces of what had taken place. At **Majdanek** near Lublin, what had started out as a POW camp in 1941 became a place of mass extermination. 150,000 were brought in – from nearly 30 countries – and around 80,000 of them (60,000 Jews) were killed. Also not far from Lublin is the Bełżec Camp, whose heinous activities cost the lives of 430,000, primarily Polish Jews, but also some who held German, Austrian or Czechoslovak citizenship. Less well-known victims were groups of Roma and Sinti people, as well as non-Jewish Poles.

Jews were transported from the train station in Koło by a goods train to Powiercie. There they were forced into lorries converted into gas chambers going to the cemetery of the **Kulmhof am Ner** camp (Chełmno nad Nerem).

247

Contemporary photograph of **the monument** sculpted by Józef Stasiński and Jerzy Buszkiewicz, unveiled in 1964 **in Kulmhof am Ner**. Beside the low relief depicting the martyrdom of prisoners reads the inscription: *We remember*.

The aforementioned **Auschwitz-Birkenau** was a complex of more than 40 places of slave labour, as well as of extermination. The three largest objects were located at Oświęcim (Auschwitz), Brzezinka (Birkenau) and Monowice (Monowitz). The orders to construct in this area were issued by Heinrich Himmler as early as in April 1940. The first "prisoners" were Poles transferred from other overcrowded places of incarceration. However, from 1941 this became a true factory of death to which Jews from across Europe were transported – men first, but then also women and children. Arrival was at once followed by a selection process resulting in the direct transfer of the vast majority to their deaths in gas chambers into which Cyclon B gas was pumped. The bodies were then removed to ovens and burnt – just one of the dreadful tasks assigned to those permitted to live on at the time of arrival and then subjected to the most exploitative slave labour. Up to the Camp's January 1945 liberation by the Red Army, 1.5 million people had been murdered here, 90% of them Jews. Today the site is a museum, as well as a place for the now-fast-fading generation of former inmates based in Israel and Poland to join the young of many countries (Germany included) on so-called **Marches of the Living**. The UNESCO listing of the Auschwitz-Birkenau Camp as an item of "World Cultural and Natural Heritage" is no mistake, but rather a deliberate attempt to remind present and future generations that human beings may be just as capable of doing unmitigated evil as they are of creating or nurturing beauty.

In the Sobibor camp died **Jews** from Poland, the Netherlands, Slovakia, the Czech Republic, Germany, Austria, France and the Soviet Union. Commemoration plaques read in eight languages: Polish, Hebrew, Yiddish, English, Dutch, French, German and Slovak.

Those murdered in Treblinka are commemorated by a symbolic graveyard made up of 17,000 rocks laid on a concrete bedrock, where over a surface area of 22 thousand m^2 the ashes of the victims are scattered.

Archive photograph showing **the halting station at Treblinka**, 6 km away from the camp. A railwayman from this station photographed the fire of the Treblinka Camp after the armed uprising of prisoners in August 1943.

Prisoners of Majdanek transporting building materials. Forced labour killed countless numbers of undernourished prisoners.

The remains of victims of **the last executions carried out in Majdanek** in July, 1944, beside the **crematoria,** before the Red Army liberated the camp. This photograph was taken after the fire, which was intended to conceal all traces of the crime.

The Mausoleum of the Victims of Majdanek, designed by Wiktor Tołkin. Beneath the concrete dome are the ashes of murdered victims.

Gypsy children, both Roma and Sinti, in a **labour camp in Belzec**, between the spring and the autumn of 1940. A year later this camp saw the implementation of the first stationary gas chambers, making use of the extermination procedures that had been carried out on the patients of mental asylums in Germany.

This pyre of rail tracks commemorates the transports of prisoners to **the Belzec** camp (Bełżec). It also resembles the pyres on which bodies were burnt.

Ohel – the mausoleum of victims of the Belzec camp was built thanks to the endeavours of the American Jewish Committee and the Government of the Republic of Poland. This photograph presents Szczelina (the Crack) – the Path to Niche, a stone wall where the symbolic names of victims have been carved.

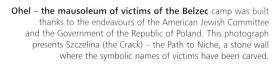

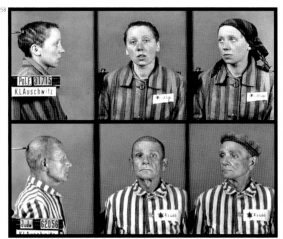

Prisoners registered in **the Auschwitz** camp (Oświęcim) had everything taken away from them, including their name, which was replaced with a number. During the registration prisoners were photographed in the same way as criminals.

A drawing by an anonymous author on the wall of the camp block in **Auschwitz-Birkenau** depicts prisoners at work. That such a work of art could have been produced in such inhuman conditions verges on the miraculous.

Interior of the women's barracks in **Auschwitz II-Birkenau**. The barracks were crammed and devoid of sanitary facilities. A soldier of the Red Army took this photograph after the camp's liberation in January, 1945.

Contemporary photograph of **the Auschwitz camp gate**. The inscription *ARBEIT MACHT FREI* (Work Makes you Free) is chilling in every respect.

11. World Cultural Heritage

The first Polish items to be listed by UNESCO as World Heritage Sites under the 1972 Convention concerning the Protection of the World Cultural and Natural Heritage were **"Kraków's historic centre"**, as officially including the Old Town, Wawel Hill complex, Kazimierz and Stradom districts, as well as (separately) the nearby **Wieliczka Salt Mine**. Both sites joined the list in 1978, and were in fact under serious threat at the time of listing. The problem for Kraków was acid rain generated by operations at the Nowa Huta steelworks and Skawina aluminium plant, as well as air pollution of various kinds inputting with air movements from over the Upper Silesia region. Once the basin in which the city lay had become heavily built up with residential blocks, aerosols present in the overlying air began to condense nitric acid, which had a major destructive influence when rain fell on the city's Wawel Castle, old tenement houses, palaces and churches. Wieliczka was not safe either. However, in 2013, the entry was extended to include the **salt mine in Bochnia**, as well as the **Wieliczka Saltworks Castle**; the name has now changed to the **Wieliczka and Bochnia Royal Salt Mines**. In 1979, Poland's first two World Heritage Sites were joined by a third located on Polish territory but certainly not Polish, as careful wording of the entry **"Auschwitz-Birkenau – the former German Nazi Concentration and Extermination Camp (1941-1945)"** makes clear. That same year, UNESCO recognised the outstanding value of a natural site – the famous **Białowieża** (Primaeval)

Forest. The **Historic Centre of Warsaw** (in fact of necessity a faithful post-war recreation of the Old and New Town districts) gained listing in 1980, precisely because it is "an outstanding example of a near-total reconstruction of a span of history covering the 13th to the 20th century". **Zamość Old Town** is in its original Renaissance form and was listed in **1992**, while the **Mediaeval Town of Toruń** followed five years after that. Toruń owes the existence of its oldest Gothic-style buildings to the presence there of the Order of Teutonic Knights that had come into Poland in 1226, at the invitation of Duke Konrad of Mazovia, who was seeking their support in evicting the pagan Prussians. The Knights rather overstayed their welcome, still being well entrenched in the early 14th century when they constructed **Malbork Castle.** WHS-listed at the same time as the Toruń site (in 1997), the Castle is Europe's largest example of a brick-built fortress from the Middle Ages, to which finishing touches were put following the arrival of the Order's Grand Master whose seat this was to become. Quite a different cup of tea is the Mannerist Architectural and Park Landscape Complex and Pilgrimage Park at **Kalwaria Zebrzydowska**, listed in 1999, and representing one of the country's major pilgrimage destinations – a place of "great spiritual significance" as the UNESCO entry has it. It has remained virtually unchanged since its 17th century funding by Mikołaj Zebrzydowski, which resulted in the establishment of no fewer than 42 chapels erected

The leafy green **ring of the Planty surrounds the Old Town in Cracow**.
This park was established in the 19th century in the place of demolished urban fortifications.

Wieliczka. The old castle was the seat of the *żupnik*, the King's official tasked with monitoring the salt mines here and at Bochnia.

St Kinga's Chapel in Wieliczka is situated 100 m below ground – it is the most impressive and opulent of the mine's chambers.

The **Bochnia** salt mine began working local deposits in the mid 13th century, continuing in operation until 1990. Today, visitors are welcome to look at the old workings, the mining installations and the galleries of salt sculptures.

between 1605 and 1616 to designs by Paweł Baudarth. Also religious, though of a different denomination, are the Evangelist **Peace Churches in Jawor and Świdnica**, listed together in 2001 as witnesses to the often stormy history of Protestant-Catholic conflict, but most especially to the efforts some made to seek reconciliation and tolerance. The frames of the buildings went up following the signing of the Peace of Westphalia ending the Thirty Years' War of 1618-1648. Other **wooden churches** of quite separate origin in the Gothic style were listed in 2003, these being scattered across the hill landscape of southern Poland's Małopolska region, in the villages of **Binarowa, Blizne, Dębno Podhalańskie, Haczów, Lipnica Murowana** and **Sękowa**. The well-preserved churches feature fine polychromy and historically important fittings. Finally (so far) come two more 21st century listings – of 2004 and 2006 respectively – which reflect the German heritage of regions returning to Poland after World War II.

The Białowieski National Park protects the most precious nature areas of the Białowieża Forest.

Auschwitz-Birkenau. The Nazi concentration and extermination camp (1941-1945). This photo shows a part of the camp, which was established in Oświęcim in 1941 by the German occupiers for Polish prisoners, which later functioned as a part of the largest death factory within the Third Reich.

Warsaw's Old Town, as seen from the New Town.

The objects in question are **Mużakowski/Muskauer Park**, as well as the **Centennial Hall in Wrocław**. The Park, today bisected by the Polish-German border, was established by Prince Hermann von Puckler-Muskau in the years 1815-1844, along the banks of the Neisse. Of such (literally) groundbreaking value was it that it served as a model of landscaping referred to on both sides of the Atlantic. The Centennial Hall in what had been Breslau likewise became Polish at the War's end, being renamed the People's Hall in 1948. Its architecture and engineering were both very innovative for their day, the 1911-1913 construction work being to a design by Max Berg. Further wooden masterpieces found their way on to the List in 2013, in the form of the **wooden Orthodox churches** (tserkvas) in the Polish and Ukrainian parts of the Carpathians at **Radruż, Chotyniec, Smolnik, Turzańsk, Owczary, Kwiatoń** and **Brunary Wyżne** (in Poland), plus **Matkiv, Drohobych, Rohatyn, Nyzhniy Verbizh, Yasynia** and **Uzhok** (in Ukraine).

The Old Town in Zamość encapsulated the Renaissance ideal of a perfect city. It was founded by Jan Zamojski, and designed and built between 1580-1619 by Italian architect, Bernardo Morando.

Toruń. The still-surviving Mediaeval street layout lined by red-roofed buildings.

Malbork – the view from the High Castle looking onto **St Mary's Stronghold**, built between 1382-1389.

Jawor. The Evangelical Church of the Holy Ghost or "Peace Church" is Early Baroque in style, and shaped like a rectangle with four levels of seating. It can accommodate 6000 people.

Kalwaria Zebrzydowska – founded by Mikołaj Zebrzydowski. This Baroque church within the Bernardine monastery was built between 1603-1609. Together with Calvary Hill, it has been a place of pilgrimage since the beginning of the 17th century.

275

Church of Peace in Świdnica. Western elevation of the beautiful half-timbered wall construction.

The interior of **the Church of the Archangel Michael in Binarowa**. Built around 1500, the church is richly adorned with Renaissance polychromes from the beginning of the 16th century and baroque polychromes from the mid-17th century.

The Church of the Archangel Michael in Dębno Podhalańskie was built in the 15th century; it is a unique example of a wooden Gothic structure with a polychrome interior.

276

A Romantic-style bridge in the eastern part of **Muskau Park** (the largest English-style landscaped park in either Poland or Germany). It represents a triumph of the 19th-century European garden-designer's art.

Hala Stulecia (The Centennial Hall) **in Wrocław** was designed by Max Berg and ceremonially opened in May, 1913. With its reinforced concrete structure, it is one of the pre-eminent examples of modern European architecture. Its design has inspired many artists.

At **Kwiatoń,** the wooden St. Paraskeva's Orthodox Church is a former place of worship of the Lemko people which was built in the late 17th and early 18th centuries on a three-square plan (chancel, nave and women's section).

Turzańsk. The St. Michael the Archangel Orthodox Church which preserves icons from 1895.

12. National Parks

The **Białowieża Primaeval Forest** is a place of survival for a patch of such original, largely-untouched forest – one of Europe's last. It was therefore listed as a World Heritage Site by UNESCO in 1979, though its valuable features had first attracted the conservatorial attentions of the Jagiellonian kings in the days of old. Likewise, when Poland fell, the Tsars of Russia made sure that care was extended to this area at least. A strict reserve was put in place in 1921, a National Park (Poland's first) following in 1932. As its emblem, the **Białowieski** (Białowieża) **NP (National Park)** has the **European bison** – a species saved from global extinction right here. Out of an area of 10,502 ha, 4747 ha enjoy strict protection. **Babiogórski NP** (of 3392 ha) protects the nature of the Babia Góra Massif – Poland's highest elevation away from the Tatra Mountains (peaking at **1725 m a.s.l.**). The forests growing on its slopes have the classic layered structure characterising altitudinal zones of vegetation. **Biebrzański** (Biebrza) **NP** affords protection to the Biebrza Valley and the **extensive marshes** within it, these offering major refuges for birds and beasts alike. This is Poland's **largest National Park** of all (at 59,223 ha). The **Bieszczadzki** (Bieszczady Mountains) **NP** takes in the highest part of the Eastern Carpathians remaining within Poland – areas in which nature gradually returned farmland into wild country. The Park extends over 29,202 ha, of which 24,696 ha is forest. **Drawieński** (Drawno) **NP** (covering 11,342 ha) protects the natural treasures of Pomerania: beech forests on morainic elevations, clean lakes, and fast-flowing rivers. **Gorczański** (Gorce) **NP** is a 7030 ha area preserving relict natural forest of what was once the Puszcza Karpacka Forest. Extending right up to the Warsaw city limits is Poland's second-largest National Park – **Kampinoski** (Kampinos) **NP**. Over its 38,544 ha, it takes in inland dunes overgrown with forest, with marshes in the depressions in between. The **Karkonoski** (Karkonosze Mountains) **NP** protects the more elevated part of the mountains in question, which represent the highest of the Sudety ranges, reaching 1602 m a.s.l. at the summit of Mt. Śnieżka. In the 1970s, acid rain fell to such an extent that forest simply died away over 570 ha here. However, this was also a reflection of the kind of forest that had been put here – a monoculture of planted spruces. Their place has now been taken by species present here naturally until the 18th century, when people decided they knew what was best. **Magurski** (Magura) **NP** takes in the most naturally valuable areas of the Low Beskid range, with beech forests and Poland's lowest sites for forest of dwarf mountain pine.

Carpets of **blooming anemones** are an early sign of the coming of spring in **Białowieski NP**.

The lynx (*Felis lynx*) is the biggest wild cat in Europe. The species of lynx living in the **Białowieski NP** is monitored by a GPS system.

The **Narwiański** (Narew) **NP** (of 15,380 ha) is termed the Polish Amazon by some, taking in the upper reaches of the Narew, whose main channel branches out into an absolute labyrinth of arms and backwaters.
The consequence is that the Park area can only be visited effectively by boat. Poland's smallest Park – the 2146 ha **Ojcowski NP** – protects incredible rockforms and other valuable natural features of the Prądnik Valley.
The **Bory Tucholskie** (Tuchola Forests) **NP** arose *i.a.* to protect a group of so-called "lobelia lakes" with crystal-clear carbonated water and a specific flora. The fantastic rock labyrinths known as Wielki Szczeliniec (at 919 m a.s.l.) and Skalniak (Błędne Skały – at c. 850 m a.s.l.) are

Białowieski NP. The European bison (*Bison bonasus*) is Europe's largest wild-living land animal. Once almost hunted to extinction, thanks to conservation measures this species is no longer endangered.

The wolf (*Canis lupus*) can be found in Poland in the **Biebrzański NP and elsewhere.** Farmers perceive the wolf as a pest, whereas foresters regard it as an ally in the selection of deer.

Covered by forest, the Red Bog in Biebrzański NP is one of the biggest peat bogs in Poland, and is home to a thriving population of elk deer.

Nesting on **the Biebrza floodplain areas** encompassing the national park are 21 endangered species of birds. The populations of some of these birds are the largest in Europe.

Since 1992 **Bieszczadzki NP** has been a part of the International Biosphere Reserve called Eastern Carpathians. This photograph presents **the valley of the upper San River of Bieszczady Mountains.**

The wide-open spaces of **Bieszczadzki NP** are ideal for mountain walks, although you may encounter wolves, bears, European bison and vipers.

View from the moraine hill overlooking **Lake Ostrowieckie** in **Drawieński NP**.

the attractions of the **Gór Stołowych** (Stołowe Mountains) **NP**. Established in 2001 (as the youngest National Park in Poland), **Ujścia Warty** (Warta Confluence) **NP** protects riparian habitats for wetland bird species over an area of 7956 ha. The **Pieniński** (Pieniny Mountains) **NP** in turn extends protection across the whole of Poland's smallest mountain massif. An area of just 24 km^2 has a record 13-15,000 animal species; while 1 m^2 of meadowland here supports some 30-40 flowering plant species. The area of **Poleski** (Polesie) **NP** (9762 ha) is almost entirely taken up by forests, lakes and marshes, these being breeding grounds for such rare bird species as harriers, curlews, black-tailed godwits, black grouse and short-eared owls, as well as reptiles like the declining European pond terrapin. The Lublin Upland is home to **Roztoczański** (Roztocze) **NP** – 8482 ha of land whose natural attributes were first protected by the Zamoyski family as early as in the 16th

The War Cemetery in Palmiry within **Kampinoski NP**.
Here during World War II Germans executed by firing squad Polish political and economic activists, as well as important public figures.

In wintertime in **Karkonosze NP** the wind, frost and damp create both fantastic snow and ice formations and leave hoar frost on trees.

century. **Słowiński NP** (18,618 ha) arose on coastland with mobile dunes adjacent to Lakes **Łebsko** and **Gardno**. It owes its name to the Pomeranian people known as the *Słowińce*. The Łysogóry, the highest range of the Świętokrzyskie Mountains (peaking at 612 m Łysica) create the backbone of **Świętokrzyski NP**, which *inter alia* protects the fir forest. The dieoff of firs has finally been arrested here following 40 years of existence of the Park. **Tatrzański** (Tatra Mountains) **NP** is the most-frequented protected area in Poland (with 3 million visits per year), and the only one in the country to support truly alpine-type relief. **Wielkopolski NP** in turn protects landforms left behind by the melting ice sheets, as do **Wigierski** (Lake Wigry) and **Woliński** (Wolin Island) **NP**, the latter located along the most picturesque stretch of the Polish Baltic shore.

Ojcowski NP, *Igła Deotymy* (Deotym's Needle) – one of the numerous rocks with an unusual shape to be found in the Prądnik Valley. It owes its form to the rainwater erosion of thick layers of limestone.

Beaver lodges – in the 1980's in **Ojcowski NP** this species was reintroduced to the Prądnik and Sąspówka rivers.

Jaskinia Ciemna (The Dark Cave) in **Ojcowski NP**. There are about 400 caves in the park, many of which are inhabited by bats.

Gravestones made of **Magurski sandstone in Łemkowski cemetery**. The resettlement of the Lemkos people in 1947 caused Lower Beskid to become a habitat for returning wildlife.

Magurski NP – a waterfall on sandstone bassets.
Sandstone is the main rock of Beskid Niski (Lower Beskid).

The rocky labyrinth at the top of **Szczelinec Wielki**, the highest peak of **the Stołowe Mountains** (919 m asl) has an abundance of fantastic rock formations. One such formation, *Małpolud* (Ape man), has become the symbol of the region.

In the **monastery on Łysa Góra** (the Bald Top) (594 m asl) a tiny fragment of wood from the Holy Cross is kept. Świętokrzyskie (Holy Cross) Mountains and **Świętokrzyski NP** took their name from this relic.

Trzy Korony (The Three Crowns) (982 m asl) – the highest mountain within the boundaries of **Pieniński NP** owes its name to the vivid arrangement of its rocky peak and the three battles for the Polish crown fought at the foot of the mountain.

This bend in the Dunajec River in the **Pieniński NP** (here seen from Sokolica, 747 m asl) is regarded as one of the most beautiful spots in Poland.

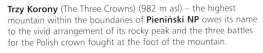

Shifting sand dunes encroaching on the forest on the sandbar of Lake Łebsko in **Słowiński NP** are a unique geological phenomenon.

The Kluki Museum of the Slovinian Village within the **Słowiński NP** presents monuments of the material culture of the Slovincian People – Pomeranian people whose speech survived here till the middle of 20th century.

The Tatra mountain region is the only area in Poland with a distinctive postglacial alpine sculpture. The photograph presents the upper part of **the Valley of the Five Polish Lakes**.

The most beautiful lake in the **Tatra Mountains NP** is **Morskie Oko** (the Eye of the Sea) which is situated in the Rybi Potok Valley at the base of the **Mnich** (the Monk), which is 2,068 m asl.

The crocus **Spisz Saffron** (*Crocus scepusiensis*) is a protected plant. Universally associated with mountain meadows, it can also found growing wild in the lowlands.

The Tatra highlanders regarded the Carline (*Carlina acaulis*) as a magic plant containing nine secret healing properties. It is a protected plant and can often be found in the folk art of the Podhale region.

Bats are the inhabitants of some of Poland's largest caves, which are located in the massifs of the Western Tatra Mountains.

Rigorously protected, **Marmots** inhabit the alpine meadows of the Tatras.

In the **High Tatra Mountains**, and especially in the Wołoszyn massif, **bears** establish their lairs. In autumn and spring they wander along the entire chain of the Tatra Mountains.

The chamois (*Rupicapra rupicapra*) inhabits the highest mountains of Europe from the Pyrenees to the Caucasus, including the **Tatra Mountains**. It is has adapted to living at high altitudes.

312

Wigry NP. Upon the surface of the Wigry Lake the silhouette of the Monastery of the Cameldolite order is beautifully contrasted against the evening skyline.

The Wigry Monastery of the Cameldolite order was built between 1704-1745 on an island that is now linked to the mainland. Cameldolite monks traditionally built their residences far from populated areas.

Woliński NP is located at the mouth of the Oder River, in North-Western Poland, and also encompasses the north-western part of Wolin Island. Moraine hills dominate the landscape, as too does its **coastal cliff-top** that stretches for 15km, and reaches 100m in places.

Lake Góreckie is delightfully situated in **Wielkopolski NP**. The total surface area of all the lakes in the park totals 447 hectares. These lakes host rich aqueous flora and as many as 35 species of fish.

314

13. Poland and Poles in art

Familiarity with a country may be increased greatly through the study of its art, most especially since this often presents people, landscapes and historical events. There are hardly any typical portrait presentations from the time when Polish art was first beginning to develop. Romanesque and Gothic portrayals were of Saints or of Christ Himself. However, we can assume that the faces of these and other figures were based on models living at the time. The column "of sinners" **in Strzelno** certainly does include secular figures, but these are entirely anonymous. One of the first known "portraits" – the epitaph of Grzegorz Wierzbięta of Branice – likewise devotes more space to the patron St. Gregory, as well as to the Virgin and Child, than it does to the man himself. The paintings by the **Master of the Dominican Passion** includes backgrounds to biblical events in the form of landscapes identifiable as ones from the artist's environment. The gallery of Polish portraiture only really begins with the Renaissance. The early 16th-century faces to the so-called "Wawel Heads" are anonymous to us now, but were clearly easily-recognisable likenesses of real Cracovians at the time. The artists then active often failed to sign their works. Thus, for example, certain pieces most likely by **Stanisław Samostrzelnik** can only be attributed to him.

The same approach was taken by **Marcin Kober**, whose portrait of Stefan Batory is of confirmed authorship, while that of the King's wife Anna Jagiellonka is not. A collective portrait of the great and good of those times is found in Hermann Hahn's *The Coronation of Mary* from the years 1623-4. The Old Polish portaiture includes likenesses of monarchs, potentates and leading lights in the Church, but also shows the merchants of Gdańsk. Portrait painting in fact developed within the Royal Court, as well as in Gdańsk, where active artists included **Andrzej Stech** (1635-1697). **Grave portraits** were also appearing across Poland, the aim being to recall the life of the dead and mark their passing. The need for them arose first and foremost from the simple fact that family members scattered across what was then the huge territory of Poland could not hope to return in time for burial services. The portrait thus "took the place" of the deceased, the nearest and dearest finding a focus for their prayers and a way of saying goodbye to his/her Earthly presence for the last time. The art-form is, furthermore, a manifestation of the trend in Polish culture known as **Sarmatism**, about which more is said in Chapter 15. The *Apotheosis of the Bonds Between Gdańsk and Poland* from the brush of **Izaak van den Blocke** (1608) offers us an easily-recognisable view of the city from the east,

This low relief on the stone **Romanesque column of the Holy Trinity Church in Strzelno** is a unique masterpiece for its representation of lay people.

On the ceiling of the throne room of **the Wawel Royal Castle** are **30 portraits** of prominent Cracovians carved before 1535 by Sebastian Tauerbach and Jan Janda.

A compilation of miniatures produced by the leading Polish artist of the Renaissance,́ Stanisław Samostrzelnik. Entitled **Liber geneseos illustris familiae Schidloviciae** (*Book of Origins of the Illustrious* Szydłowiecki Family (1532), which presents a genealogical record of the noble family of Krzysztof Szydłowiecki. The Kórnik Library.

The monumental altar of **the Oliwa Cathedral** with paintings by **Andrzej Stech**. In the background of this painting dating from 1683 Stech depicts monks of the Cistercian Abbey.

as well as a realistically conveyed landscape of the Vistula Mouth and Baltic shore in the direction of Kępa Orłowska. More frequent examples of urban landscapes realistically conveyed only began to appear with the *vedute* by **Bernardo Bellotto,** which depict mid and late 18th-century Warsaw. The return to nature characteristic of the **Romantic Period** ensured much more regular portrayal of Polish landscapes. Music also offered its own special kind of depiction. While **Chopin** (who was born at **Żelazowa Wola** in the Mazowsze region in 1810) was an opponent of grand-scale depictions of reality using music, instead considering his art a pure and non-presentational one, it remains hard for the Polish listener of his mazurkas or ballads to not detect references to the countryside by the Vistula, some passages proceeding like willows along some country road, while others bring to mind a skylark rising up above some open field. In the 19th century, the Polish mountains, and most especially the Tatras, became a major inspiration for *plein-air* painting. The work of **Józef Chełmoński** was likewise motivated by the landscapes

Lay and clerical dignitaries of the Republic of Poland kneeling before **Hermann Hahn's** "Coronation of the Virgin Mary" **in the Cathedral in Pelplin,** a work that is recognised as the most splendid expression of Marian Piety from 17th century Poland.

Hermann Hahn's "The Baptism of the Pomeranian Prince Subisław" **in Oliwa Cathedral.** Here the painter presents events from 1170 with the protagonists attired in 17th century dress.

Coffin portraits, both male and female, kept in treasury of the Gniezno Cathedral.

Castrum Doloris (Castle of Grief) – the catafalque decoration modeled on ancient Roman custom was customary for Polish Sarmatian art in the 17th and 18th centuries.

Sculptures on the western elevation of the **Wilanów Palace**, glorify the political and military achievements of Jan III Sobieski.

of the plains of Mazowsze, that other heartland of Poland. **Jan Matejko** turned his attention to the presentation of **Polish history's great events**. Portrait painting was also flourishing, though it had to face tough competition from mid-century due to the emergence of the cheaper alternative of **photography**. Indeed, it was not long before photography went over from being a form by which to document the world to something far more artistic. The Impressionists also went out into the open air, though landscapes were just one inspiration behind 20th-century art. The face was by then coming to be treated as a pretext for art, as one may observe in the work of the "**S.I. Witkiewicz Portrait Company**". The 20 inter-War years saw the gradual coming-together of avant-garde groupings, while other currents and trends also made themselves felt. Poland's highly-diversified Modern Art drew on varied sources of inspiration and utilized diverse means of expression. Post-1945, artists built on the pre-War avant-garde traditions and trends as regards colour, though further artistry involved the development of yet more new ideas, including conceptualism and expressive figurativism using new materials, technologies and media.

Isaak van den Blocke's plafond ceiling painting "The Glorification of Connections of Gdańsk with Poland" in **the Town Hall of the City of Gdańsk**.

Collection of portraits of **the Wiśniowiecki Family** to be found in **Wilanów Palace**.

An everyday scene from **eighteenth-century Warsaw**: "The New Town Market Square and the Church of the Sisters of the Blessed Sacrament" – by **Bernardo Bellotto** "Canaletto" (1721-1780), who worked in Warsaw from 1767 onwards. In Poland he was referred to as Canaletto due to his familial and artistic relationship with the famous Venetian, Antonio Canale.

"Portrait of Apolonia Poniatowska" by Marcello Bacciarelli (1731-1818), who was the court painter of king Stanisław August Poniatowski.

"Portrait of Pelagia Sapieżyna" by **Elisabeth-Louise Vigée-Lebrun** (1755-1842), a French painter, who produced more than 600 portraits of European monarchs and members of the aristocracy.

Chopin's grand piano in Ostrogski Castle in Warsaw. The castle is the seat of the National Institute of Fryderyk Chopin.

Outbuilding of the Skarbek palace **in Żelazowa Wola, where Frederyk Chopin was born and spent his childhood.** Work to convert this building into a museum in honour of the composer began in 1928.

"Rejtan", one of the great **historical paintings by Jan Matejko** (1838-1893), depicting an event from 1773 when Tadeusz Rejtan, a member of the Polish Assembly, tried to prevent the Assembly from accepting the partition of Poland.

Portraits of Jan and Marusia Kasprowicz by **Stanisław Ignacy Witkiewicz -Witkacy** (1885-1939). Both Jan Kasprowicz, poet and translator, as well as Witkacy, prose writer, dramatist, painter and the philosopher, resided in Zakopane.

"Mountain Landscape" by Wojciech Gerson (1831-1901) is a late work and was inspired by the wild beauty of the Tatra Mountains.

Zdzisław Jasiński (1863-1932), **"Spring"**, oil on canvas from 1908. Educated in Munich, Jasiński introduced symbolic and allegorical motifs into his paintings.

"An Angel" by **Jacek Malczewski** (1854-1929), one of the most highly regarded symbolist painters of the Young Poland period.

The most controversial painting of the Polish symbolist era, **"The Frenzy of Rapture"** by **Władysław Podkowiński** (1866-1895), which represented a reaction against aesthetic canons.

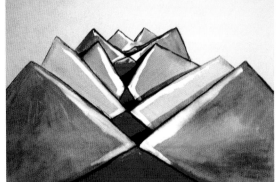

"Red Mountains" by **Andrzej Wróblewski** (1927-1957), painted in the year of the artist's tragic death during an expedition in the Tatra Mountains.

"AC80", painted by Zdzisław Beksiński (1929-2005). Painted in 1980, this painting is as alarming as the rest of the painter's oeuvre, and is on display in Sanok Castle. Sanok was the hometown of the artist.

"King Bull" by **Teresa Pągowska** (1926-2007). In the line forming the horizon we can see the outline of Tarnica (1346 m asl) in the Bieszczady Mountains.

14. Romanesque and Gothic art

Poland's acceptance of Christianity ensured that the artistic and building talent founded on Slav roots was augmented by the Romanesque art and architecture then being created in the Christian countries. There thus began to appear – alongside the settlements with their earthworks and heavy timber – **stone churches** (also often with a secondary defensive function), as well as large residences known as *palatia*. Sadly, it is now very largely only archaeological finds that can tell us about what was built in Gniezno and Poznań, at Ostrów Lednicki and **on the Wawel Hill** in Cracow. The **rotunda in Cieszyn** is the oldest surviving structure, from the late 11th or early 12th century, built from limestone slabs. However, the walls of many of the early Romanesque buildings had been made use of as later buildings went up, examples here being the **Church of St. Adalbert** in Cracow, or the Benedictine Abbey in Tyniec. Also surviving through to our era in larger number are the Romanesque buildings erected in the 12th century. **St. Andrew's Church in Cracow**, the **collegiate church at Tum near Łęczyca**, and the churches in **Inowłódz**, **Czerwińsk** and **Inowrocław** all attest to a pretty high level of architectural attainment in the then Poland. The 13th century brought a definite further flowering of the Romanesque, the difference being that brick began to be used alongside stone (as in **Sandomierz**

and **Kościelec Proszowicki**). These changes were very much a reflection of approaches being taken by the religious orders, above all the Benedictines and Cistercians, whose missions were accompanied by higher culture at **Koprzywnica** and **Sulejów**, for example. Other kinds of Romanesque art have survived alongside the architecture in buildings. The churches and monasteries in **Jędrzejów** and **Wąchock** attest to this, and there are examples of sculpturework in the form of the **columns in the church at Strzelno**, the **portal at Ołbin**, the famous **Gniezno** (Cathedral) **Doors** and **Płock Doors**; a few examples of painting, illuminated books and manuscripts, and various golden items plus jewellery. Gothic art, which found its way to Poland (initially in parallel with the Romanesque) in the 13th century, disseminated the idea that brick was a favoured building material, and also encouraged the use of the technological innovations of the day (*inter alia* the pointed arch, cross-rib vaulting and buttresses). All of these made it possible to build both lighter and taller. Silesia is particularly noteworthy here, with its Gothic churches and Ostrów Tumski cathedral in Wrocław, for example; as is the city of Gdańsk, in which Poland's largest place of worship up to the 20th century was erected. While Gothic-style **churches** may be relatively widespread across the whole

St. Mikołaj's Chapel in Cieszyn is a Romanesque rotunda dating from the turn of the 12th century, preserved on the site of the original castle, and then the castle of Cieszyn princes.

St. Andrew's church in Cracow was built in 1079. Extended around 1200, it became a shelter for townspeople during the Tartar invasion in 1241.

The Foundation Tympanum, presenting Maria Piotrowa Włostowicowa and Świętosław Piotrowic offering the church under construction to the Mother of God, is situated in the internal side portal of the Church of **the Blessed Virgin Mary in Piasek, Wrocław**.

of Poland, defensive structures of the period are best represented by the **castles in Silesia**, and along its one-time border, as well as **in Prussia**. Silesia owed its initial fortification to the Piast Dukes. Later, when Czech rulers from the House of Luxembourg took power (from 1335), King of Poland Kazimierz the Great put powerful lines of defence in place along the then border. The castles forming them (today mainly in ruins, thanks to the Swedish incursions of the 17th century) became the subject of a 20th-century process of establishing networks of tourist trails, such as the "Eagles' Nests" trail and that of the "Jura Fortresses". It was (and is) said of King Kazimierz that he came to the throne in a wooden Poland and left behind a country made of stone. Indeed, the monarch invested huge sums in his defensive infrastructure. No fewer than **53 castles and town fortifications** were put in place during his reign.

The interior of the nave and presbytery of the stone **church of St. Prokop in Strzelno**, erected from granite slabs between the years 1125-1210.

The stone **basilica in Tum near Łęczyca** was built between the years 1141-1145. Bombarded in 1939, the basilica was rebuilt between the years 1947-1954 with its Romanesque forms having been restored.

The Romanesque **Church in Inowrocław** came into existence at the turn of the 13th century. In a ruinous state since 1779, it owes its present condition to restoration work carried out in 1901 and 1950.

Stone parts of the Annunciation of the Blessed Virgin Mary's Church in Czerwińsk on the Vistula date back as far as 1150. The brickwork was added in the 15th and 17th centuries.

This richly carved **portal** from 1138 was made for St. Vincent's Church at Ołbin Abbey of the Benedictine monks. After the abbey was destroyed in 1526, half of the portal was fitted into the southern wall of **the Wrocław church of St. Mary Magdalene** dating from the 16th century.

The concentration of the Gothic-style castles in the north of Poland reflects the settlement there of the Teutonic Knights. They founded their fortresses on territory they had wrested from the pagan Prussians. The finest example of one of the Knights' strongholds is of course **Malbork Castle**. Other interesting Gothic-style buildings include the **Town Halls** in Gdańsk and Toruń, as well as Tarnów and Sandomierz, though the latter were enriched by Renaissance elements in the 16th century. Gothic sculpture (virtually all religious) is still present in churches, as well as in museums. There are **altars,** with the Veit Stoss piece in St. Mary's, Cracow, to the fore, various **Madonna and child** examples, and **crucifixes** showing Christ's suffering and death in a naturalistic way. An important current to Gothic art is the painting, which assumes various forms from the impressive polychromy on the walls of churches and temporal buildings, via **altar paintings** (of the Cracow School), through to **illuminations** and **miniatures** in hand-decorated books. Various smaller handmade items also appeared at the time, in particular monstrances, chalices and reliquaries.

The Cistercian Abbey in Sulejów was founded by Kazimierz Sprawiedliwy (the Just) in 1176. The best-preserved part of this Romanesque architectural complex is the stone-brick church of St. Thomas, built before 1232.

Part of **the Płock Doors**. The originals are in the Orthodox Cathedral of St. Sophia in Veliky Novgorod, Russia, but faithful copies can be seen in Płock.

Made around 1170, **the Gniezno Door** in the south portal of the Cathedral in Gniezno presents 18 scenes from the life of St. Wojciech.

Goblet from the cathedral treasury room **in Gniezno** with an opulent Byzantine bowl made of agate dating from the end of the 10th century. The gilding was executed at the end of 12th century.

Codex aureus, the "golden code" – a decorative book written by hand in gold letters on specially coloured parchment; exhibit from the Archdiocesan Museum **in Gniezno.**

A transcribed sheet from a 15th century **Bible** from the collection of the Pauline monastic library **in Jasna Góra, Częstochowa.** The ornate initial of the First Royal Book depicts the duel between David and Goliath.

Openwork cornice adorning the wall of the Gothic **Cathedral of St. John the Baptist in Wrocław.**

The Gothic **Cathedral of St. John the Baptist** was built after 1244 on the site of an earlier Romanesque building destroyed during the Tartar invasion. Its characteristic silhouette dominates the skyline of **Wrocław**.

St Mary's Church in Stargard in West Pomerania is recognised as one of Baltic region's the most outstanding masterpieces of Gothic architecture.

The Town Hall of the Main City of **Gdańsk** (as seen from Long Street) was built in stages between the years 1327-1556. Damaged by fire in 1945, it was rebuilt between the years 1946-1954 and 1964-1970.

Wrocław – the largest Gothic Town Hall in Poland, built in stages from the end the 13th century, acquired its fundamental shape between the years 1470-1480.

The ruined castle in Mirów, dating from the 14th century, once defended Silesia's Polish border. It was destroyed in the Swedish Deluge of 1655.

The Cathedral in Frombork was built between the years 1329-1388 on a fortified hill. Nicolaus Copernicus was a canon of the local chapter. He died in Frombork in 1543 and was buried beneath the cathedral floor.

Episcopal Castle in Lidzbark Warmiński built between the years 1355-1401 fell within Polish boundaries in 1466. The Episcopal throne of Warmia was occupied by people such as: Enea S. Piccolomini – later Pope Pius II; Marcin Kromer – an eminent historian and humanist; and Ignacy Krasicki – the poet, as well as many representatives of the ruling European dynasties, such as: the Batorys, the Wazas and the Hohenzollerns.

General **view of the castle in Malbork**. Built between the years 1280-1393, it was the main seat of the Great Masters of the Order of Teutonic Knights from 1309 till 1466. Once taken over by Poland, it became the seat of the royal starosts.

Gothic triforia of galleries surrounding the castle courtyard **in Malbork**.

Malbork: the richly carved **portal called the Golden Gate** leads from the galleries of the High Castle to the chapel of the Blessed Virgin Mary. The figures are those of **the "Foolish Maidens"** from the parable featured in St. Mathew's gospel.

The beautiful Madonna from St. Mary's Church in Gdańsk is the work of an anonymous sculptor who was active in the first quarter of the 15th century.

Decorative motif on a 15th century bowl of **the baptismal font from the parish church in Bnin** near Kórnik in Wielkopolska.

The central box of **the late-Gothic triptych** dating from the beginning of the 16th century, which can be found in **the Church of the Blessed Virgin Mary on Piasek Island in Wrocław,** presents Mary, the Mother of God, St. Catherine and St. Barbara.

The Blessed Virgin Mary falling asleep – the central scene of the altar sculpted by Veit Stoss **in the Mariacki Church in Cracow.** The sculptures carved in linden wood are of giant size; the figure of St. Peter's supporting Mary is 280 cm tall.

The Gothic **Piéta from St. Mary's Church in Gdańsk**.

Crucifix from the altar of the southern nave of **the Mariacki Church in Cracow**, which was sculpted by Veit Stoss in 1491. The cross and the body of Christ are made from one block of stone.

Late-Gothic **epitaph** chiseled by Veit Stoss in **the Dominican Church in Cracow** dedicated to Callimachus (Fillippo Buonaccorsi), the tutor of the royal sons and one of Poland's earliest exponents of Italian Renaissance thought.

A vision of Hell in a scene from the Last Judgment from the medieval polychrome uncovered in our times from under a layer of plaster in **St. Johns Church in Toruń**.

15. Pearls of the Renaissance and the splendour of the Baroque

Renaissance cultural influences from Italy reached Poland in the 15th century, though the style did not really have its full flowering here until the 16th. The beginnings may be perceived in the **remodelling of Cracow's Wawel Castle** under King Zygmunt the Old – work entrusted to *Florentinus Italus* of Florence, **Bartolomeo Berrecci** and **Maestro Benedykt**. At the same time, painter **Stanisław Samostrzelnik** (1490-1541) was active at the Cistercian Monastery in **Mogiła**, painting both miniatures and murals. The Early Renaissance phase (1500-1545) was characterised by the building on to the Wawel cathedral of the so-called **Zygmuntowska Chapel**, as well as by the increasing popularity of tomb sculptures. The style came to establish an independent identity between 1545 and 1575, Polish culture entering a golden age at that time. Indeed, the Polish language was adapting itself for full use as a tool in artistic expression, even if the academic world was still keeping faith with Latin. Many printed books began to appear, while practitioners of Renaissance art now began to extend well beyond the then capital of Poland, appearing in Lvov (today's Ukrainian Lviv), Lublin, Warsaw, Poznań and Silesia. **Poznań** obtained a fine New Town Hall between 1550 and 1560, while the **Castle at Niepołomice** was made over in the Renaissance style, the **Cloth Hall** in Cracow gained an attic decorated with mascarons and the **Collegiate Church in Pułtusk** was constructed. The Piasts ruling in Silesia had **Giacoppo** and **Francesco**

de Pario working for them, as well as **Andreas Walter I**. The leading sculptor was **Jan Michałowicz of Urzędów**, a pupil of Giovanni Cini and Giovanniego Maria Mosca known as the Paduan (*Padovano*). The tomb of Bishop Filip Padniewski was sculpted by the latter in 1575, and thus exemplifies the art of the Renaissance's second phase in Poland. The style flourished in the years 1575-1640, before fading away by virtue of the transition into Mannerism and later Baroque. The latter period is best personified by master **Santi Gucci**, who won the patronage of the Myszkowski and Firlej families, as well as ultimately the King. Gucci's studio was in Pińczów, conveniently close to the deposit of Kielce Marble. Perhaps an even greater patron of the style was Count Zamoyski, who commissioned **Bernardo Morando** to design a whole town layout for what would be dubbed **Zamość**. It is to Morando that we owe the town's still-extant Collegiate Church, Town Hall, Zamoyski Palace and *Akademia* building. So influential was the architectural achievement here that others drew on it, as in buildings erected across the Lublin region in the early 17th century. **Gdańsk** takes a separate place in the story of the development of 16th century Polish art. The Gothic style hung on here longer than elsewhere, almost immediately giving way to Mannerism. The Baroque style so widely seen in Poland came here with the Jesuits, whose first involvement in Polish architecture yielded the **Church of Saints Peter and Paul in Cracow**, as modelled on

In the beginning of the 16th century Poland's first Renaissance painter **Stanisław Samostrzelnik** adorned the walls of **the Cistercian Church in Mogiła near Cracow** with his paintings.

The Renaissance **Royal Wawel Castle,** which was built during the Jagiellonian dynasty, became a model for many Polish Renaissance buildings.

Zygmuntowska Chapel by Wawel Cathedral is regarded as the finest architectural Renaissance masterpiece north of the Alps.

Rome's *Il Gesú*. Post-1630, the Baroque work carried out in the country drew on (and drew in) a series of other influences – Italian, obviously, but also native Polish and even Flemish (via the work being done in Gdańsk). The impact was sufficient to establish a distinctive variant of the style, to be seen to this day across all the lands that are – or were once – Polish. Kielce Marble had to compete with black marble from Dębnik near Cracow, and alabaster was also widely used. Stucco and other ornamental plasterwork represented a new artistic medium at this time. The creators of the Polish Baroque can be identified as **Giovanni Trevano** (d. 1644), to whom we owe the aforementioned Peter and Paul Church, **Baldassare Fontana** – behind the decoration of St. Ann's in Cracow; Dutchman **Tilman van Gameren** (1632-1706), who was ultimately ennobled in recognition of his life's work; **Andreas Schlüter** of Gdańsk (1659-1714), whose output may be admired in Berlin and Saint Petersburg as well as Poland, and Pole **Kasper Bażanka** (1680-1726), who worked in Cracow and across Małopolska. The Counter-Reformation exerted a major influence on

The Gate of Legnica Castle, which was the seat of the Piasts of Legnica-Brzeg, the last line of the first Polish dynasty.

Decoration on the facade of **the gate to the castle** of the Legnica-Brzeg princes **in Brzeg**. On top, the busts of the Piasts, on the bottom, prince Jerzy II with his wife, Barbara Brandenburska.

Poznań Town Hall's ceiling, supported by pillars, was adorned in a post-Renaissance mannerist style.

Jan Michałowicz of Urzędów made **the gravestone of Bishop Andrzej Zebrzydowski in the Wawel Cathedral** between the years 1562-1563.

Attributed to Santi Gucci, **the Kryski family gravestone** in St. Stanisław's Church **in Drobin** in western Mazovia was sculpted in the second half of the 16th century.

The Master from Szamotuły, **"The Annunciation" – a votive painting** by Łukasz Górka, the bishop of the Kujawy region, who died in 1542, and whose image can be found in the lower part of the painting. The Kórnik Library.

the process by which Baroque art was shaped, even offering wholly new forms of expression. **Gothic-style churches were refitted with Baroque-style altars** pretty much *en masse*, while many **interiors** were also subject to the same process. The exquisite examples from **Lower Silesia** are noteworthy. Secular art was also in full bloom, Baroque influences being detectable in park layouts and palace designs, of course, but also in the richly-decorated facades of town houses and country manors; as well as in the art adorning their interiors. It was also at this time that a Polish nobility searching for its origins hit upon the idea that their ancestors might have been the Sarmatian warriors who did battle with the Romans. The idea took root, and *Sarmatism* (artistic references to the said **Sarmatian culture**) coincided with the Polish Baroque era. Fusing features from east and west, the trend's most unique manifestations were its very well-developed funeral ceremonies (assuming solid form in a mania for **grave**

One of Poland's most beautiful Renaissance **town halls** was built **in Chełmno** between the years 1567-1572. At present it houses the Museum of the Chełmno Region.

A marble **ciborium**, the work of Giovanni Maria Mosca, called Padovano – **in the Mariacki Church in Cracow.**

The Market Square and the Town Hall in Zamość, an example of Renaissance architecture created on the basis of open-space urban planning.

The Renaissance **castle** of the bishop of Cracow, Piotr Myszkowski, built between the years 1585-1595 **in Książ Wielki** in Małopolska, probably according to the design of Santi Gucci.

portraits), as well as the emphasis placed on the Cult of the Madonna, as exemplified by pilgrimages to the **Jasna Góra Monastery** near Częstochowa. So well-built was the latter Baroque structure that it successfully resisted the Swedish siege of 1655. More utilitarian manifestations of Sarmatism in turn include what are now deemed the "classically Polish" outfits of silk worn by noblemen.

The Golden Tenement by the Long Market **in Gdańsk**, designed by Abraham van den Blocke in 1609. This tenement building belonged to the merchant family of Gdańsk patricians, the Speymans, whose motto was: *Do not fear, be just!*

The fortified **residence** of the Krasicki family **in Krasiczyn** was built in stages between the years 1598-1618. Finials of the castle walls are decorated with attics in the so-called *Polish attic* style, which originated in the area of Lublin at the beginning of the 17th century.

Completed in 1615, **the St. Michael and St. Christopher Tenements in Kazimierz Dolny** belonged to the Przybyło merchant family. It's particularly notable for its richly ornamented attics.

Polish architect, Kasper Bażanka, designed **the Piarist Church of the Transfiguration in Cracow,** and Moravian artists, sculptor Christian Bola, and illusionist painter Franciszek Escstein adorned its interior.

Built under the supervision of Giovanni Trevano between the years 1609-1619, **the Church of St. Peter and St. Paul** on Grodzka Street **in Cracow** is the earliest Baroque church in Poland.

Jerzy Eleuter Siemiginowski painted *St. Anna Samotrzeć*, which is located on the high altar of **St. Anna's church in Cracow,** whose interior was in turn designed by Baldassare Fontana.

Święta Lipka, the Catholic sanctuary built in the evangelical Duchy of Prussia between the years 1687-1693. The church has an outstanding organ, and since the end of 1980's on every Friday in July and August concerts are held here.

At the end of the 18th century, Jan Niezabitowski covered the interior of the Baroque **wooden church in Goźlin** with illusionist polychrome. The church itself was built between the years 1769-1776.

Stucco decoration of **the Knight's Hall in the Leszczyński family palace in Rydzyna**. Between the years 1705-1709 this palace was the residence of king Stanisław Leszczyński.

Jan Reisner painted the plafond **"Morning Star"** after 1683. The painting adorns Queen Marysieńka's study in Jan III Sobieski's **Wilanów Palace**.

The Krasiński Palace in Warsaw was built between the years 1688-1699, under the supervision of Tilman van Gameren.

Built in the early 17th century for Stanisław Lubomirski by Maciej Trapola, **Łańcut Palace** is unquestionably Poland's finest aristocratic residence. In 1816, on the death of Princess Izabela Lubomirska's the whole estate became the property of her grandson, Alfred Potocki I. The Palace remained in the Potocki family until the outbreak of World War II.

The stairwell of the **palace** of Michał Radziejowski (designed by Tilman van Gameren) **in Nieborów** is covered with locally manufactured ceramics, modeled on famous products from Delft.

Giacomo Scianzi adorned **St. Elisabeth's Chapel in Wrocław Cathedral** between the years 1680-1700.

The Cistercian **Abbey in Henryków** in Silesia was founded in 1222. Between the years 1682-1709 Matthias Steinl produced magnificent Baroque sculptures for the Abbey church.

This mural fresco by Michael Willman (often called the Silesian Rembrandt) was painted between the years 1693-1698 on the wall of **St. Joseph's Church in Krzeszów**, and depicts the Flight of the Holy Family into Egypt.

Franz Joseph Mangoldt sculpted adornments for the Hall of the Princes of the Baroque **monastery in Lubiąż** in Lower Silesia between the years 1734-1738.

Baroque monstrance from the Pauline **Church on the Rock in Cracow.**

Baroque woodcarving – a fragment of the monumental wooden altar in the post-Cistercian monastic church **in Kamieniec Ząbkowicki.**

The majestic polychromes painted by Johann Kuben
in the late-Baroque Jesuit church of **the Rising
of the Holy Cross in Brzeg**.

"The Adoration of the Shepherds",
the altar painting by Hermann Hahn, which he painted
for the presbytery altar **in Oliwa Cathedral**.

Abraham van Blocke and Jan Strakowski made this marble-alabaster
gravestone for banker **Szymon Bahr, and his wife, Judyta,
in St. Mary's Church** in Gdańsk between the years 1614-1620.

The Church of the Assumption in Krzeszów. Examples
of decoration: a Regency "grid-pattern" and a stylized Rococo motif.

16. From Neo-Classicism to modernity

The onset of Poland's **Age of Enlightenment** coincided with the 1764 accession to the Polish throne of King Stanisław August Poniatowski, the country's last monarch. The fact that these new intellectual trends were the subject of royal patronage would soon become clear, as artistic and architectural styles underwent a sea change. Warsaw was the greatest single beneficiary of the King's interest. Court Architect **Jakub Fontana** (1710-1773) was a designer of Baroque-cum-Neo-Classical buildings who also adapted to the Rococo style readily enough. However, fully-fledged Neo-Classicism was practised by Fontana's successor, **Domenico Merlini** (1730-1797), as influenced by the King himself, plus Merlini's co-worker of the next generation, **Jan Christian Kamsetzer** (1753-1795), who was in receipt of a royal scholarship. It was Fontana and Merlini who made over the interiors of Warsaw's Royal Castle, though their best known work is the Łazienki Park-Palace complex. Forms perfected in the last days of independent Poland continued to serve in to the 19th century. They were used, for example, in the years 1818-1822, as **Jakub Kubicki** was working on the redesign of *Belweder* for the Russian Governor of the Congress Kingdom. Perhaps the greatest practitioner of Neo-Classicism was **Antonio Corazzi** (1792-1877), who was invited to Poland by the Kingdom's authorities and worked in Warsaw between 1819 and 1847. His designs include the city's opera house or "Grand Theatre" (1825-1833). In 1821, Corazzi was joined by fellow Italian **Henryk Marconi** (1792-1863), who came to regard Poland as his second homeland. Marconi's designs include, the terminus of the Warsaw-Vienna Railway (1844-1845). The Polish lands partitioned off by the Prussians gained at least something from that, as Berlin architect **Karl Friedrich Schinkel** (1781-1841)

designed such buildings as the splendid Kamieniec Ząbkowicki Castle, St. Martin's Church in Krzeszowice, Kołobrzeg Town Hall and the Palace of the Archbishop of Gniezno. It was also on the basis of a Schinkel design that the old Kórnik Castle gained a wonderful new lease of life. The second half of the 19th century is primarily associated with the erection of large industrial complexes, as well as with resort to **earlier historical styles**, most especially Neo-Gothic, Neo-Renaissance, Neo-Baroque and Eclectic. The greatest single example is provided by Łódź, which some encyclopaedias dub Secessionist. In truth, the **Secession** left a certain number of typical interiors in the city, but only a couple of buildings genuinely attributable to the style. Cracow does feature a number of interesting buildings that are genuinely Secessionist, plus other items from the late 19th and early 20th centuries harking back to other historical trends. Located in the Austrian sector of partitioned Poland, Cracow was able to enjoy at least a taste of the rich artistic life characterising the *Belle Epoque* – hence such fine buildings from those days in the city's Retoryka, Smoleńsk and Piłsudskiego Streets. The 20 inter-War years saw architectural form simplified in the direction of Functionalism. Good examples of the work of the day are to be found in **Modernist** Gdynia – a port constructed from scratch at that time. Destruction, rather than construction, characterised the tragic years 1939-1945, with rebuilding perforce conducted in the **Socialist Realist** style prevailing from 1945 to 1956. Central Warsaw continues to live with the consequences, as does the now-much-visited industrial town on the edge of Cracow called Nowa Huta (the name means simply "New Steelworks"). Yet Socialist Realism was actually the high-point for architecture in the Polish People's

The royal architect, Domenico Merlini and the royal grant holder, Jan Christian Kamsetzer, designed and adorned **the Great Hall of the Royal Castle in Warsaw** in 1777.

Domenico Merlini brought his own style to bear on **the Royal Library of Stanisław August** when he designed and adorned it between the years 1779-1782.

The classical **Palace of the Potocki Family in Natolin** with its half-open columned hall was built between the years 1780-1783.

The classical **Królikarnia Palace**, situated on the edge of the Vistula valley, is also a testimony to the mastery of Domenico Merlini. The place hosts a Museum of Sculpture named after Xawery Dunikowski.

The decorative painting on the ground floor of **the Natolin Palace** of the Potocki family has been preserved.

Republic, that which came after being of mostly lower standards, with the skills of urban planning boiling down to the arranging of rectangular blocks across the landscape, in lines or not in lines. Back then, the chances of success for any design with more than a hint of innovation were vanishingly small, the exceptions being whatever the Catholic Church was able to fund. Some modern places of worship of genuine artistic worth were erected – in the face of implacable official opposition – most especially at Nowa Huta, where the struggle to build the Lord's Ark Church is now legendary. Another fine item from that period is the Church of the Lord's Ascension in Warsaw's Ursynów residential district, which was begun in 1982. The transformation that swept the Eastern Bloc 7 years later left architects free, and their work took a wide range of paths. Some returned to the traditions of inter-war architecture, others moved into Post-Modernism. Poland's architectural metamorphosis has since proceeded apace (in cities in particular), yet the dull concrete legacy of the barrack-like housing estates must inevitably dog the country for decades to come. Thankfully,

Designed by Jakub Kubicki for the tsar's brother, grand duke Konstanty, **Belvedere Palace** was built between the years 1818-1822. On November 29th, 1830 rebelling cadet officers barged into his chambers, initiating the November Uprising.

The Classical **ballroom of the royal Palace on the Island** in Łazienki in Warsaw was the work of Jan Christian Kamsetzer.

Palace on the Island – the main architectural feature of **the park-palace complex of Łazienki**, built for Stanisław August, who never saw the final work of his architects, having remained in Petersburg after his abdication.

The Teatr Wielki "Great Theatre" in Warsaw is Antonio Corazzi's *opus magnum*. It was built between the years 1825-1833, and having been destroyed in World War II, was rebuilt between the years 1951-1965.

Designed by Antonio Corazzi **The Palace of the Treasury on Bankowy Square in Warsaw** was built in the period of the Congress Kingdom of Poland, established in 1815 at the Congress of Vienna.

The Monument of prince Józef Poniatowski in front of the presidential palace in Warsaw. The bronze statue, cast by Bertel Thorvaldsen, was destroyed in 1944. The present statue was cast from forms that had been kept in the artist's museum in Copenhagen.

Working in Denmark, Poland and Rome, Bertel Thorvaldsen (1768-1844) was a master sculpture. He sculpted **the Nicolaus Copernicus monument in Warsaw**.

beyond all the grey anonymity, world-class designs are beginning to appear. Warsaw might be an example, already playing host to the *Metropolitan* building by Lord Foster, and now seeing a start put to the construction of a new tower designed by Daniel Lieberskind. The contest for the city's new Museum of Modern Art has in turn been won by Venezuelan-born Swiss architect Christian Kerez.

The Neo-Gothic **Castle of Marianna Orańska in Kamieniec Ząbkowicki** was built between the years 1838-1865 according to the design of Karl Friedrich Schinkel and Ferdinand Martius.

The outstanding Prussian architect, Karl Friedrich Schinkel (1781-1841) worked extensively on Polish territory in the period of the Partition of Poland. **The Church in Krzeszowice** is one of the 60 buildings in Poland designed by Fredrich.

The Mauritanian room in the palace in Kórnik was modelled on the Alhambra palace courtyards in Granada, Spain. The room is a home to many works of art and national treasures collected by the Działyński family.

The neo-Gothic **Church of St Joseph**, with its tower modelled on the bugle-call tower of the Mariacki Church, was built between the years 1905-1909. Designed by Jan Sas-Zubrzycki, it was erected on the Podgórski Market Square (Foothill Market Square) **in Cracow**.

The neo-Renaissance **manor house of Artus in Toruń** was built at the end of the 19th century on the site of an earlier Gothic dwelling that had been demolished 1802.

Completed in 1902, **the dining room in the palace of the industrialist, Israel Kalmanowicz Poznański in Łódź** was adorned in the Italian style.

The Mauritanian Room in the palace of the Łódź industrialist, Karol Scheibler. This palace was the second building in the world (after the Eiffel Tower) to have an electrical lift installed.

Cracow's new urban theatre (today named after Słowacki), opened for the public in 1893, is one of the first theatres in the world equipped with electric lighting powered from its own generator.

The Art Nouveau interior decor of a **swimming pool in Wrocław** corresponds to the ancient Roman hot baths.

This fairy-tale **castle in Moszna near Opole** was built between the years 1896-1914, incorporating the walls of the Baroque palace.

Teodor Talowski (1857-1910), designed **the house "Pod Śpiewającą Żabą" (Under the Singing Frog)** on Retoryka Street **in Cracow**.

The flowery ornamentation of the facade of a **Warsaw tenement** on Lwowska Street.

A sunflower was a popular decorative motif at the turn of 20th century. This photo presents a fragment of the facade of the Art Nouveau **tenement in Brzeg**.

An eclectic Art Nouveau **tenement building** on Mokotowska Street **in Warsaw**.

The Art Nouveau **trading house** of Schlesinger & Grünbaum Company built in 1901 **in Wrocław**. The designer Leo Schlesinger used an external reinforced concrete structure installing the huge windows.

Stanisław Wyspiański (1869-1907) designed the stained glass and interior decor of **the Medical Society building in Cracow**. Wyspiański frequently used leaves and flowers as decorative motifs in his designs.

The interior decor of the auditorium of **the Chamber of Commerce and Industry in Cracow** was designed by Józef Mehoffer (1869-1946), who incorporated folk ornamentation into his design, which correlated with the search for a Polish national style in architecture and design.

Art Nouveau motif crowning the building of **the Palace of Arts** of Szczepański Square **in Cracow**.

At the turn of the 20th century artists looked to make every single object into a work of art. Exhibit items from **the Art Nouveau collection** in the Mazovian Museum **in Płock**, witch features everything from bedroom furnishings to the wing of a paravan screen.

Designed by Oscar Sosnowski, **St Roch's Church in Białystok** was built thanks to votive offerings following the regaining of Poland's independence. The work began in 1927 but stopped for the duration of the war. It was finally completed in 1947.

The modernist **Church of the Sacred Heart of Jesus in Cracow**, built for the Jesuits between the years 1909-1921, is a monumental church with a coherent vision in terms of its architectural design and it paintings and sculptures.

The city of Gdynia, built between the years 1922-1936, is characterized by its functional urban architecture.

Socialist realist architecture was supposed to be "national in form and socialist in content" – and so, **the attics of the Palace of Culture and Sciences in Warsaw** hark back to Poland's Baroque period.

Facade of **Warsaw's MDM building**, which is a decorative example of Polish socialist realism.

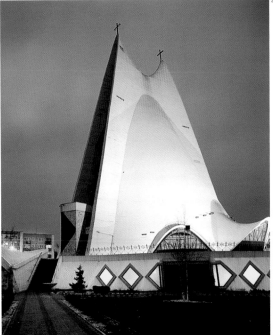

The 8-metre tall figure of the Crucified Jesus in **the Nowa Huta Church of the Mother of God**, Queen of Poland, is called *the Ark of the Lord*. On the day of its consecration (May 15th, 1977) 70,000 people attended mass at the church.

The concrete "M" shape of the **Church of God's Mercy in Kalisz**, consecrated in 1993, corresponds to the word Mercy.

"The cross became the gate" – this quotation from the poem by Cyprian Kamil Norwid inspired Marek Budzyński, the designer of **the Church of the Ascension** in Ursynów **in Warsaw**.

The shopping centre **Złote Tarasy** (The Golden Terraces) **in Warsaw** is an example of how a commercial building can achieve artistic dimensions. and have a positive impact on the landscape of the city.

The charming **Krzywy Dom** (Crooked House) **in Sopot**: when seen in a photograph it looks like a trick of the camera, whereas when seen with one's own eyes, it suggests a need for corrective glasses.

17. The birth and life of *PRL*

Polska Rzeczpospolita Ludowa (the People's Republic of Poland) was a non-sovereign state run by the communist party in Poland. It all began in 1944, when Stalin installed a puppet pseudo-government in Lublin, this muscling in on entitlements still legally possessed by the Polish authorities in exile. Poles were promised a free vote on their new situation, but the results were falsified. Thus "the people's government" lacked legitimacy, being propped up by Soviet military strength *inter alia* manifested in the presence of large numbers of Red Army personnel on Polish soil. The ugly side of the new regime was made clear in its first 12 years (1944-1956), there being brutal suppression of all opposition, with show trials, political prisoners by the tens of thousands and a determined effort to undermine the Catholic Church. On the economic side, industry, trade, schools, hospitals, pharmacies and theatres were all nationalized. Land was handed out to peasants, while "collectivization" brought the founding of the State Farms. The "thaw" of 1955 followed Stalin's death in 1953 and denoted a certain easing of the repression, though the situation reversed in the wake of workers' protests in Poznań. Nevertheless, a change was signalled by the release of **Władysław Gomułka** from prison (where he had been held for deviations of a reactionary right-wing and nationalist nature – as the jargon had it). Gomułka became head of the Polish United Workers' Party (PZPR), and presented his programme for a "Polish Road to Socialism". The Red Army remained, though now present by virtue of a signed agreement "between allies". The terror subsided rather, the political detainees released at this point including Primate of Poland Cardinal Stefan Wyszyński. The 12-year period running from 1956 to 1968 inclusive thus came to be dubbed the era of **limited stabilisation**. There was a moderately just distribution of the deprivation countrywide, while

some things the authorities did even won popular support (the extension of **electricity supplies into rural areas** being one example). Disturbances flared up once again in March 1968, when student street protests were catalysed by the cancellation (as "requested" by the Soviet Embassy) of a performance of Adam Mickiewicz's *Forefathers' Eve* (a drama of 1832 portraying the life Poles lived under the Tsar). The *Milicja* engaged with the crowds in the most brutal fashion, reminding waverers that the "Polish Road" differed little from others. Wishing to save face, Gomułka followed his national socialist instincts and blamed the Jews. He sought **to turn society against "Zionists",** prompting the emigration of thousands. The 12-year period 1968-1980 was one in which society perfected civil disobedience, while the authorities pursued irresponsible economic experiments. The latter (commenced with under Gomułka) involved price changes that provoked a swift reaction from protesters in the coastal cities. The ultimate death toll associated with these protests was at least 44. Gomułka had to go, and his successor, **Edward Gierek,** proceeded with the building of the socialist paradise … on the basis of loans from the Capitalist West! Living standards did rise, though a system absorbing more than it could give back was doomed to collapse, as it did in 1976. Further price manipulations provoked yet more workers' protests, and the again heavy-handed *Milicja* played into the hands of pioneer civil rights organisations. Then, in 1978, came the news that a **Pole had become Pope.** Karol Wojtyła's triumphant homecoming as John Paul II compelled the authorities to hear the voice of the Catholic Church. Strikes of summer 1980 led to the establishment of the **Solidarity** trade union, a huge workers' movement independent of a Party that had theoretically been representing their interests for years. The period 1980-1992 kicked off with 15 months of relative

An appointee of Stalin, Bolesław Bierut governed Poland between the years 1944-1956. Like the majority of dictators, he liked to be photographed with children.

454

Destroyed during the war, post-war Poland required prompt **reconstruction**. The communists exploited this situation by implementing a system of "socialist rivalry in work", in that ideological incentives replaced economic ones.

Investments in heavy industry saw the **construction of places like Nowa Huta** (the New Steelworks) **near Cracow**, which were also intended to support the munitions industry.

Soviet architecture also proved influential in post-war Poland, wherein **socialist realism** was fused with Polish elements. Here we see the pedimented attic of a building in Nowa Huta.

freedom of speech, brought to an abrupt end on 13th December 1981, when **martial law** was declared and an authoritarian government under Gen. **Wojciech Jaruzelski** took power. **Lech Wałęsa** was awarded the Nobel Peace Prize in 1983, at a time when the authorities were pursuing a limited reform programme that promoted the role of the private sector somewhat. Meanwhile, **Ronald Reagan** had a policy of his own **to bring down the Soviet Union.** The crude murder by security operatives of the Solidarity chaplain, **Father Jerzy Popiełuszko,** persuaded Poles just how little their rulers had changed, and the priest's funeral turned into one massive anti-government demonstration. However, as the arrival of the **Gorbachev era** of *perestroika* in the USSR had consigned to history the Brezhnev Doctrine, General Jaruzelski could only respond to ongoing protests by agreeing to the **Round Table Talks** that bore fruit in June 1989 elections that were basically free (if reserving some seats for the communists). The opposition won and an end was put to rule by the Party. The old system was in fast retreat, the PZPR being disbanded in January 1990 and the name People's Republic dropped. However, Gen. Jaruzelski continued as President for almost another year, and it was only on May 8th 1991 that **Soviet forces began to pull out**. The first fully free elections took place on 27th October 1991. In the June of the following year, the secret services archive from the old system came under wider scrutiny – launching a process that would taint political life for years. Nevertheless, by 2004, Poland was sure enough of its sovereignty to offer open support for the Orange revolution in Kiev.

Somewhat ironically, **the Central Headquarters of the Communist Party was converted into the Warsaw Stock Exchange** after the fall of Communism.

Józef Cyrankiewicz (first left) was Poland's longest-serving Prime Minister and Deputy Prime Minister (1947-1970), while **Władysław Gomułka** (in glasses) was First Secretary of the Communist Party in the years 1956-1970. It was on their orders that workers' protests along the Polish coast were suppressed bloodily in December 1970 (at the cost of several tens of lives).

May Day marches were organized during the Communist era and workers were required to participate in the celebrations. In the photograph we see the Warsaw May Day march of 1970, seven and a half months before the Gdańsk riots.

Edward Gierek (first from the left), the party leader between the years 1970-80, proposes a toast with party activists beside yet another fine socialist structure. Prime Minister Jaroszewicz is standing beside him.

General **Wojciech Jaruzelski** (middle) never proposed a toast with alcohol, as he officially promoted abstinence. Restrictions on alcohol and the ban of its sale before 13.00 hrs led to an increase in sales.

Demonstration against the imposition of Martial Law. The V-shaped sign was supposed to symbolise the anticipated victory of Solidarity, which had been driven underground.

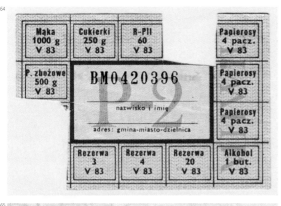

The food ration coupon for flour, butter, sweets, cigarettes and alcohol. There were also ration coupons for meat, which were highly sought after in Communist Poland.

A 100 zloty banknote in 1980 could buy you either a half a litre of vodka or 25 loaves of bread. Ten years later this note had the value of one empty envelope without either stamp or glue.

Monument to the victims of the NKVD (the communist police) and UB (the Polish secret police) murdered in the Stalinist prison in Warsaw's Praga district. It was built between the years 1997-2001 in the place where the prison had been situated.

Banners of the de-legalised Solidarity unfurled during **a mass being celebrated by Pope John Paul II** in Gdańsk on June 12th, 1987.

Patriotic protests in Cracow organised on September 17th, 1989, on the 50th anniversary of the Russian invasion of eastern Poland.

Fr. **Jerzy Popiełuszko**, a Solidarity activist, murdered by officials of the state police force.

Commemoration ceremony by **the grave of Fr. Popiełuszko** on the anniversary of his death.

18. The *Solidarity* Phenomenon

The anger and disillusionment felt by Poland at the December 1970 Government decision to raise food prices assumed its most dramatic form along the coast. On **December 14th**, a march took place in **Gdańsk**, heading down from the Shipyard to the HQ of the Voivodship Committee of the Party (PZPR). Somewhat ironically, the Polish United Workers' Party did not speak to protesting workers on that day, and in fact opened fire from one of the windows on the following day. The protesters' tempers frayed, and they torched the Party Building, also igniting a wave of "incidents" throughout the city. On December 16th, the response from the Army came as Gdańsk Shipyard employees leaving work were fired on, as was the workforce heading for the morning shift at the railway station in next-door Gdynia. Undaunted, the rebels became active in **Szczecin** on **17th December**, while orders to open fire on unarmed citizens were also given by the communist authorities in Elbląg. Ultimately, the suppression of workers would require 500 tanks and 700 armoured cars, as well as 5000 members of the *Milicja* and 27,000 soldiers of the People's Army. The total number of civilian victims would seem to have been at least 44 (though sources differ), and witnesses claim to have seen people run over by the tanks. This was in fact the largest-scale massacre perpetrated against the workers of Poland by those purporting to represent their interests. The ensuing "palace coup" at Party Headquarters with the removal from power of Gomułka did not resolve the matter. Strikes went on until February 1971 (longest in Łódź), at which point the old prices for food were actually restored. However, May 1st 1971 saw workers taking the opportunity offered by the celebration marches of that day to pay homage on a unfurled banner to the victims of the previous December. Nevertheless, it would not be **until 1976 that more pronounced unrest again surfaced.** The trigger was an effort to raise prices, but the more organized workers' response represented the first steps on the road to the founding of free trade unions. The ultimate **emergence of "Solidarity" in 1980** was encouraged by a dissatisfied public obtaining support from the Catholic Church at home, as well as the teachings in Poland and around the world of its then Polish head, Pope John Paul II; by a policy of opposition organisations seeking to operate legally; and by bitter memories of the bloodthirsty measures the authorities had been prepared to resort to. Also of significance were the steady breakdown of an economic system divorced from market realities and the failed policies of Leonid Brezhnev. In the popular imagination, the tangible food shortages in summer 1980 reflected transfers to Moscow, at that time host-city of the Olympics.

Blazing **building of the Regional Committee** of the Polish United Workers Party **in Gdańsk**, set on fire by workers in December 1970.

471

Archive photo of **the street fights** which took place **in Gdańsk** in December 1970.

So strikes broke out again, first in Lublin, these making it impossible for the communists to celebrate another year in power. In August, a strike at the Gdańsk Shipyard was launched to defend free trade union activists Anna Walentynowicz and Lech Wałęsa. The Strike Committee demanded that their dismissed colleagues be allowed to return to work, that permission be given to erect a monument in honour of the December 1970 victims, that the legality of the strike weapon be recognised, that pay be increased, and that welfare payments available to the children of ordinary workers be equivalent to those paid out to offspring of *Milicja* members. Discussions with management brought a proposal that the shipyard workers might indeed obtain a payrise were they to return to work

Banner demanding that due reverence be given to shipyard workers killed during the December events. This banner had been prepared in secret and unfurled during a march which took place **on May 1st, 1971.**

Lech Wałęsa, who would go on to be chairman of Solidarity and later president of Poland, speaking to the families of striking shipyard workers gathered at the shipyard gate **in August, 1980.**

An archive photograph of **the ramp in the Gdańsk shipyard**, which bore the name of Lenin at the time of the anti-Communist labour movement.

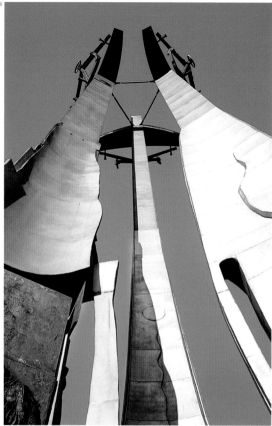

Monument to the miners of the Wujek Coalmine in Katowice, who were shot dead by ZOMO – the Polish riot police, during a strike protesting against the imposition of Martial Law in Poland in December, 1981.

Gdańsk crosses – **monument to the victims of December 1970**. Designed by engineer Bogdan Pietruszka and a team of artists, and executed by shipyard workers, the monument was unveiled on the 10th anniversary of the massacre.

An archive photograph showing a police cordon stopping a protest convoy of buses and lorries organised by the transport union members of Solidarity, **(3-5 August, 1981)**. The intervention of the authorities caused **a three-day traffic blockade in the centre of Warsaw.**

– and there were some activists moved to accept that offer. However, the overall feeling was one of "solidarity" with the employees in smaller industrial concerns with less muscle. An **Inter-Works Strike Committee** came into being, its **list of 21 demands** now being recognised by UNESCO as a key element of world cultural heritage embraced by the "Memory of the World" Programme. The **strikes spread nationwide**, and the agreements that ended them provided for the establishment of the *Solidarność* Independent Self-Governing Trade Union. Yet the existence of an independent organisation 10 million strong was inherently incompatible with the communist system. Furthermore, the Solidarity Rally held in Gdynia in autumn 1981 bore fruit in an appeal to the workers of other communist countries

Cracow – the summer of 1981. A demonstration organised by Solidarity demanding the release of arrested political activists.

John Paul II's third trip to Poland in June 1987 coincided with the economic and political disintegration of the entire Communist system. This photograph shows the Pope being made welcome by **the citizens of Warsaw**.

Pins worn by members and sympathizers of Solidarity. Above – the official trade union emblem from the period of the union's legal activity. Below – an underground pin commemorating Lech Wałęsa's winning of the Nobel Prize for Peace in 1983.

Issued in free Poland, **a Solidarity commemorative coin** of a nominal value of 100,000 zlotys. It also recalls the hyperinflation, which came with the collapse of Communism.

to follow suit by establishing their own free trade unions. The by-then drastic steps of **delegalising Solidarity** in the wake of the introduction of martial law in December 1981 did not restore the monopoly of power communists could once have counted on. Rather, the underground union organisations continued to influence work crews in different industries, and were able to mount protest activity – as when workers turned out en masse for the funeral of Father Jerzy Popiełuszko in autumn 1984. A next wave of **strike action in spring 1988** forced the authorities back into dialogue. And, as the Polish example did indeed prove capable of effecting change in neighbouring countries, freedom ultimately emerged throughout Central and Eastern Europe.

A Solidarity demonstration infront of by the St Stanisław Kostka Church in Żoliborz, Warsaw in the early 1990s. This was a period of dynamic social, economic and political changes in Poland.

19. Polish customs and traditions

Polish customs arose out of **a linkage between Slav and Christian traditions**, including under the influence of yet **other cultures**. The course followed by the Polish year of celebrations runs parallel to that of the Catholic Church. The first period of that year is **Advent**, followed by **Christmas** as Winter gathers strength. December 6th is **St. Nicholas's Day**, offering the opportunity for Father Christmas to make his first of two present-delivering visits to Polish children (and not only). Now known worldwide, the habit of **decorating a Christmas tree** came to Poland too, replacing an earlier one whereby single green branches were brought in as decoration. **Christmas Eve supper** should by rights be commenced with at dusk (as the first star appears). Though a meal of many courses, it is technically still a fast, hence a dominance of dishes made with flour, mushrooms, vegetables and fish. The sending of cards is practised, though on nothing like the scale in Anglo-Saxon societies. Family **carol-singing** continues to go strong. Boozy **New Year celebrations** are said to go back to the year 1000 (the times of Pope Sylvester), when the people of Rome went wild with relief that the world had not ended at the millennium. The Epiphany celebration of January 6th ushers in the period known as *karnawał*, which resembles the Carnival times known from other countries. At this time it is OK to play hard and eat plenty. February 2nd marks **Candlemas** – or the feast of candlelight associated with the Virgin Mary. On that day, crowds are to be seen carrying lighted candles back home from church. The Carnival period comes to an end with **Shrove Tuesday** (*Ostatki* in Polish). On this Day, children in fancy dress would sing songs to neighbours in the hope of receiving loose change or something sweet to eat – above all a doughnut. The day for doughnuts is nevertheless the last Thursday in Carnival, i.e. *Tłusty Czwartek* (Fatty Thursday – a kind of *"Jeudi Gras"*). **Ash Wednesday** marks the first of 40 days of **Lent**, whose Polish name *Wielki Post* means "Great Fast". **Palm Sunday** celebrations resemble those elsewhere, if with Polish-style "palms" comprising bunches of spring twigs, dried coloured grasses, etc. The precise form depends on the region, as does the size (sometimes impressive – contests are even held). **Easter** is a movable feast. As elsewhere, there are celebrations on Maundy Thursday and Good Friday ("Great" Thursday and Friday in Polish), as well as Easter Saturday and Easter Day. Easter Monday is celebrated more faithfully than in some other countries, *i.a.* for reasons given below! While the outline plan of events is that set by the Church, regional differences and specialities also apply – as for example when a Good Friday **mystery play** is performed at Kalwaria Zebrzydowska (whose name makes reference to Calvary). All Poland participates in the traditional blessing (sprinkling with Holy Water) of a basket containing food and a decorated egg on Easter Saturday. Probably more temporal than spiritual is the habit of sprinkling (sometimes soaking) allcomers with water on Easter Monday. In some places, the ritual is pursued in folk costume. The same would certainly be true of the very solemn **Corpus Christi procession**, wherein the priest carrying the monstrance with the Holy Host beneath a canopy has his way round the parish

The Christmas tree decorated with glass balls, paper stars and coloured paper chains. The custom of sharing the wafer and exchanging blessings are important moments of the Christmas celebrations.

In some villages families **sing Christmas carols** at home **on Christmas Eve**. Carol singers also go from house to house to sing in return for a gift.

484

485

St. Francis of Assisi and his followers acted out the first Nativity play. Many homes in Poland place a manger under the Christmas tree.

Jellied carp is a mainstay of the **Christmas Eve** supper.

Makowiec – or Poppy-seed cake – is a poppy-seed filling wrapped up in a yeast pastry.

sprinkled with flower petals. Corpus Christi is the last Holy Day of the year whose date is tied to Easter. A sight readily seen in May is of young girls in white dresses and little boys in smart suits, a sure indication that the season for children to take **First Communion** has arrived (this being an event distinct from Confirmation). Summer is a time of ease for city-dwellers, hard work for country-folk. Yet both groups participate with equal enthusiasm in the **mushroom-picking** mania of late summer and autumn. Since many species are consumed, great skill is required to ensure that edible species are separated from the often-very-similar poisonous types. The obsessive interest seems not to be dimmed by fatalities that occur when one of the more deadly species is consumed in error. July and August see the **Baltic beaches thronged with people**. However, many others head south, the Madonna-cult centre of **Częstochowa** attracting pilgrims from across Poland, many of whom have made their way on foot. The first pilgrimage of this kind set off from Warsaw in 1711. With time, other cities joined in, and recently faithful from neighbour countries

Iced doughnuts, stuffed with jam or preserves are eaten on "Fat Thursday", just prior to the beginning of Lent.

In **Tokarnia in Małopolska Palm Sunday is** celebrated by the leading of a wooden figure of Christ on a donkey.

The competition for the longest **Easter palm tree** originated in **Łyse in Kurpie** and takes place every Palm Sunday throughout Poland.

A scene from **the Passion** performed on Good Friday in **Kalwaria Zebrzydowska** near Cracow.

In the village of **Górka Klasztorna** in northern Wielkopolska local farmers play biblical figures in the performance of **the Passion of Christ**.

have also been attracted. In September, another **year-class begins its school career** – something associated with the allaying of nerves with gifts of sweets – in Silesia, at least. Various commemorations of the Second World War also take place in autumn, and all the departed are remembered on **All Saints Day** (November 1st), scenes remarkable to foreign eyes involving mass visits to cemeteries, in which graves are bedecked with flowers and candles. Families gather at the last resting places of their loved ones, often heading home for a commemorative meal – for traditional eating accompanies all Poland's high days and holidays. And, though very largely Catholic, Poland also has followers of other religions, each adding to the national mix the colour and interest associated with their own customs, festivities and commemorations.

In Poland Easter food baskets are traditionally full of *pisanki* decorated eggs: or *kraszanki* (painted eggs without no decorative elements). Also added to the basket are bread, meat or a sausage, some sweets and salt.

A girl with an **Easter basket** (food to be blessed), in a garland of first spring flowers.

Baba – a **yeast cake** with raisins, baked in a special tin, graces the Easter table.

Żurek – **Easter soup** made from soured rye flour, served with hard-boiled eggs and sausage. In some regions it is the same as white borscht.

The members of folk ensemble "Sieradzanie" **playfully pouring water** over one another, which is an **Easter Monday** custom.

On Easter Monday – **"Easter Revellers"** throw water over passers – by in the village of Dobra near Limanowa.

Siuda-baba, a custom associated with Easter Monday, preserved in the **Wieliczka** region. It is said to date as far back as pagan times.

For some unknown reason, in Poland the guards of the tomb of Jesus are called *the Turks*. In the village of **Gniewczyna near Łańcut** a large troupe of guards turn out in extravagant uniforms.

119

The participants of a **Corpus Christi procession in Podhale** dress in their traditional folk costumes for the occasion.

On **Corpus Christi the procession** with the Holy Sacrament walks over flowers that have been scattered on the ground. **In Spycimierz** the procession walks over a carpet that has been arranged from flowers.

Corpus Christi processions **in the Łowicz region** are colourful affairs. In the photograph we see a group of children from **Złaków Kościelny** carrying a basket of flower petals dressed in regional costumes.

One of the four altars on the itinerary of a Corpus Christi procession in the village of **Ząb in Podhale**.

Girls dress in traditional costumes for their **First Communion**. Boys usually get their first suit on this day.

The faithful gathered on August 15th at **the Marian Sanctuary in Licheń** to celebrate **the Assumption of the Blessed Virgin Mary**. August 15th is also called the Herbaceous Mother of God day.

Warsaw pilgrims in front of the Church of the Pauline monks, setting off on foot to **Jasna Góra in Częstochowa**.

Powązki Cemetery in Warsaw. In Poland people of all religions visit family graves on **All Saints Day,** which falls on November 1st.

20. Polish cuisine

Back in the early 12th century, the French Benedictine *Gallus Anonimus* noted in his Chronicles how Piast had prepared a feast of pork and beer for the ritual cutting of his son's hair that in Slav tradition represented a boy's move into manhood. In turn, at the court of Bolesław the Brave (who ruled from 992 to 1025), the cooking was based around "manifold kinds of fowl and game", out of which "dishes from every kind were brought to his royal table". Inevitably, meat made a far less frequent appearance in peasant kitchens, the staple there being various kinds of cooked grits, very often served with milk. Use was also made of peas, as well as what the forest had to offer, particularly various fungi, honey and berries. Coarse fish also formed part of the diet from the earliest days, their better-tasting marine counterparts being a rarity indeed (as *Gallus* confirms) – at least until King Bolesław the Wrymouth conquered Pomerania in the early 12th century (though the old habit stuck anyway). The variant of cuisine characterising Polish lands inevitably began to evolve and diversify, for example as religious orders moved in from Western Europe, and as German settlement proceeded in the 13th century. Indeed, a true globalisation of food preferences took root as long-distance movements began to intensify. The **first great culinary revolution** that can clearly be dated came in the 16th century, when Bona Sforza came up from Milan to marry King Zygmunt the Old. For example, the bundle of stock vegetables upon which Polish soups are based are known collectively as *włoszczyzna* (the name meaning "Italian food"). Perhaps surprisingly, their use represented a radical departure from tradition. The various soups based around a mixture of meat and vegetable stock appeared, with the "Royal" **chicken broth** known as *rosół* to the fore: *on a low flame boil poultry and beef with carrots, parsley root, celeriac, leek, Savoy cabbage and a single baked onion plus black pepper, in water salted to taste, until a transparent broth with oily droplets floating on the surface is obtained.* The broth was – and is – served with pasta, itself present in Polish cuisine through the Italian influence. **Cabbage** also came up from the south, proving such a hit that the dish of spiced sauerkraut in which meat is first steeped and then cooked with a little red wine – otherwise *bigos* – is pretty much the Polish national dish. The description of the preparation of *bigos* in the Adam Mickiewicz epic *Pan Tadeusz* is one of the "most delicious" fragments of Polish literature. On the other side of the coin, several comestibles developed on Polish soil also proved special enough to achieve international renown. The delicacies in question are **Toruń gingerbread** and **Gdańsk vodka** (*Goldwasser*). Another major royal influence came along as France's Henri of Valois ascended the throne as Poland's first elected King in 1573. French methods – and the habit of eating with a fork – lasted far longer here than Henri himself, who returned less than a year into his reign to become King of France. Nevertheless, his country's influence dominated fashionable cuisine – as so much else

The kitchen in a mediaeval castle had to be very spacious in order to feed the large numbers of people residing within its walls. In the photo we see the kitchen **in Malbork castle.**

The kitchen of a burgher's home at the turn of the 18th century differed little to those found in mediaeval times. In the photo we see **the Uphagen home in Gdańsk.**

510

511

Steak *tatar* – raw minced beef and a raw egg yoke served with finely chopped onion, and finely chopped pickled mushrooms and cucumbers.

Smalec, "the rich man's butter" is lard from rendered pork fat. The secret of *smalec*'s taste lies in the seasoning, such as apples, onions, and herbs.

– across Europe through the 17th and 18th centuries, notwithstanding the **second revolution in Polish cooking** attributable to the potato, first cultivated in this region as recently as at the end of the 18th century. The noble tuber made up for lost time, however, soon becoming a dominant force in folk cuisine as: a) a key ingredient of starters and side dishes like potato salad, or as served with sausage, herring or peas, as well as in their jackets with butter and herring; b) a base for potato, pea, vegetable and other soups; c) a constituent of such main dishes as *kluski śląskie* (Silesian potato dumplings) in sauce, green dumplings, potato pancakes, roast potatoes with bacon or Ruthenian *pierogi* (made from mashed potato and white cheese and served with lard-fried onions); d) accompaniments to meat, served mashed, boiled, baked or fried (alone or along

Just as in mediaeval times, **thick bean soup over *kiełbasa* and bacon** goes great with beer. These days it is also served with potatoes.

Various **pastas and dumpling** dishes are central to a lot of Polish cuisine, not to mention kneaded pastry with the addition of boiled potatoes.

The kitchen of a small manor house in Russów at the beginning of the 20th century, belonging to the family of Maria Dąbrowska, one of Poland's great writers. She described this kitchen in her novel *Nights and Days*.

The village of Zalipie is famous for its custom of painting everything in a flowery ornamentation. In such a colourful kitchen even an ordinary meal must taste great.

Tomato salad, alongside **crispy lettuce and *mizeria* from fresh cucumbers soaked in sour cream.** And in winter there's always sauerkraut salad.

***Rosół* (chicken broth)** is served very hot; therefore you eat it slowly blowing on your spoon. So it is okay for men when eating *rosół* to take off their jackets and loosen their ties.

with flour); e) the source of the flour and starch in the blancmange- or custard-like desserts known as *budyń* or *kisiel* (even though these once involved cereal flours).

The Ruthenian *pierogi* represent just one of the many dishes typical of Poland that are described using the word in Polish, notwithstanding the fact that several dishes are actually being referred to. The most typical kind resembling large ravioli are served with grits, meat, meat and cabbage, cabbage and mushrooms or mushrooms alone (the collection of these from the forest being a national obsession come late summer and autumn). *Pierogi* also come in dessert versions, with cherries, fruits of the forest, white cheese, cream and sugar, etc. The list is endless, though it is perhaps best to spare the poor

The colour of this elegantly served stewed ***bigos*** shows that it has been prepared with the addition of game and seasoned with red wine.

Poland is the Kingdom of dumplings. Here we have **dumplings** in the company of **potato dumplings, stuffed potato dumplings and stuffed pancakes**.

Roasted pork ribs with new potatoes sprinkled with fresh dill (... who in such a moment would ever think about calories or cholesterol?).

***Golonka* – pork knuckle** tastes delicious when cooked in beer, and is best washed down with a shot of ice-cold vodka.

Toruń Gingerbread – exhibit on display in the Copernicus Museum in Toruń. Decorative gingerbread forms were made of wood or, more rarely, fired from clay.

The Gingerbread Museum of Toruń is part of the bakery on Rabiańska Street, which has been open since the 16th century. Visitors to the museum can see gingerbread being made in accordance with its original recipes, and by bakers dressed in 16th century attire.

Łowicz cutout from the open-air ethnographic museum **in Maurzyce** depicting a scene from a peasant wedding with guests sitting at a set table.

reader, who will doubtless be heading for the kitchen already! Of course, there is nothing to take the place of home cooking, and Poles "eat out" to a far more limited extent than their counterparts in other countries. There is a high-quality and vastly varied cuisine to be enjoyed over here, even if Poles themselves do much to encourage the stereotype that little else is available barring *schabowy* – i.e. **pork escalope with cabbage and potatoes**. Not that there is anything wrong with this fine and tasty dish, which itself represents an fusion of Slav tradition with what was brought in by the two culinary revolutions referred to.

A rarity for initiates, **flaki** is soup made from the thinly sliced intestines of a cow's stomach**.** Its preparation takes a couple of hours.

Cold trotters, or **zimne nóżki,** is a dish of meat and vegetables in jelly, and it tastes best with a squirt of lemon juice.

Potato pancakes and cream – nothing to add, nothing to take away.

Freshly dug up **potatoes** should be brought in from the field straightaway so that the sunlight doesn't turn them green.

Home-made pickles and preserves, in either vinegar or sweet sauce, are often served to guests as snacks with meats and cold cooked meats.

Home compotes are prepared in summer and in autumn and stored in the larder in sealed jars, so that when winter comes it is still possible to quench your thirst with a fresh fruit drink. Beats any drink you'd ever buy in a shop.

Table glass, such as a toasting glass from the beginning of the 18th century, from the collection of the Royal Castle in Warsaw.

Hungarian wine was once highly esteemed in Poland. It was served in this type of a **mug set with coins**. A Polish product from the around the first half of the 18th century.

Neo-gothic dining room in **Kórnik palace**.

Poland is a country that produces and consumes **home-made fruit liqueurs, liqueurs, beer and mead**… and not just vodka.

Oscypki – cheese made of ewe's milk in the Tatra Mountains, a **regional product of the Podhale**. It can also be smoked.

Pâtés – in the 18th century, in wealthy households one servant was tasked solely with preparing pâtés.

Fried bone pork cutlet coated with breadcrumbs served with sauerkraut and boiled potatoes soaked in fat loin. This dish took about 900 years to perfect.

Dining room maintained in the style of the Podhale region in **the Zakopane villa "Under the Fir Trees – Pod Jedlami"** built in the years 1896-1897 according to the design of Stanisław Witkiewicz (Witkacy's father).

POLAND

text
GRZEGORZ RUDZIŃSKI

editing and graphic design
BOGNA PARMA

photographs and reproductions
CHRISTIAN PARMA

with
BOGNA PARMA (282, 378, 382, 403, 406, 409, 410, 424, 435, 437, 438, 448)
LECH ZIELASKOWSKI (83, 100, 262, 267, 268, 312, 418, 460, 474)
WIT HADŁO (245, 246)
JACEK KOZIOŁ (GAZETA KRAKOWSKA) (85, 242)
FILIP ZIĘBA (308, 309)
GRZEGORZ RUDZIŃSKI (481)

and
THE FotoRzepa PHOTOGRAPHIC AGENCY (461, 462)
THE NATIONAL DIGITAL ARCHIVES (48-50, 455)
THE HISTORICAL MUSEUM OF GDAŃSK (12, 13, 471-473, 475)
THE CRACOW HISTORICAL MUSEUM (8, 78, 222, 223, 456)
THE JEWISH HISTORICAL INSTITUTE (224-228, 231, 250)
THE PARMA PRESS ARCHIVE (454, 464, 465)
THE AUSCHWITZ-BIRKENAU MEMORIAL AND MUSEUM (230, 258, 260)
THE REGIONAL MUSEUM IN TOMASZÓW LUBELSKI (255)
THE STATE MUSEUM AT MAJDANEK (252, 253)
THE MUSEUM AT THE FORMER CHEŁMNO EXTERMINATION CAMP (229, 247)

owners of objects
THE KÓRNIK LIBRARY (Polish Academy of Sciences) (4, 7, 317, 383, 534)
THE MAZOVIAN MUSEUM IN PŁOCK (336-338)
THE HISTORICAL MUSEUM IN SANOK (341)
THE TATRA MUSEUM IN ZAKOPANE (339)
THE DISTRICT MUSEUM IN TORUŃ (335)
PRIVATE COLLECTIONS (340)

map
MARIUSZ SZELEREWICZ

translation
JAMES RICHARDS, BARRY KEANE

dtp
Wydawnictwo PARMA PRESS
Olga Baranowska, Eliza Dzienio

printing and binding
Drukarnia READ ME, Łódź, Poland

Wydawnictwo PARMA PRESS
05-270 Marki, al. Józefa Piłsudskiego 189 b
tel./fax (22) 781 16 48, 781 16 49
e-mail: wydawnictwo@parmapress.com.pl
www.parmapress.com.pl

ISBN 978-83-7777-021-4